# TRUTHFORLIFE®

THE BIBLE-TEACHING MINISTRY OF **ALISTAIR BEGG**

The mission of Truth For Life is to teach the Bible with clarity and relevance so that unbelievers will be converted, believers will be established, and local churches will be strengthened.

## Daily Program

Each day, Truth For Life distributes the Bible teaching of Alistair Begg across the U.S. and in several locations outside of the U.S. through 1,800 radio outlets. To find a radio station near you, visit **truthforlife.org/stationfinder**.

## Free Teaching

The daily program, and Truth For Life's entire teaching archive of over 2,000 Bible-teaching messages, can be accessed for free online and through Truth For Life's full-feature mobile app. Download the free mobile app at **truthforlife.org/app** and listen free online at **truthforlife.org**.

## At-Cost Resources

Books and full-length teaching from Alistair Begg on CD, DVD, and USB are available for purchase at cost, with no markup. Visit **truthforlife.org/store**.

## Where to Begin?

If you're new to Truth For Life and would like to know where to begin listening and learning, find starting point suggestions at **truthforlife.org/firststep**. For a full list of ways to connect with Truth For Life, visit **truthforlife.org/subscribe**.

## Contact Truth For Life

P.O. Box 398000 Cleveland, Ohio 44139
**phone** 1 (888) 588-7884   **email** letters@truthforlife.org
 /truthforlife   @truthforlife   **truthforlife.org**

Is This It?
© The Good Book Company, 2019.
Reprinted 2019 (twice), 2020.

Published by:
The Good Book Company

thegoodbook.com | www.thegoodbook.co.uk
thegoodbook.com.au | thegoodbook.co.nz | thegoodbook.co.in

ISBN: 9781784983314 | Printed in Denmark

Design by André Parker

"'Is this it?' is a question most of us have asked ourselves at some point. In a truthful, personal and humorous way, this book answers that question. Rachel masterfully communicates the joys and challenges we face in our twenties, and intertwines biblical truths which we can stake our lives upon. If you are in your twenties or know someone who is, read this book."

SHAR WALKER, Author; Speaker

"An extremely helpful and timely book for younger Christians who are trying to make sense of life and faith. As a pastor of a congregation filled with young folks going through the 'quarter-life crisis', I now have a resource to give to these young believers. Is This It? is rooted in the Bible, saturated with a gospel worldview and a real pleasure to read. I wholeheartedly recommend it."

TONY MERIDA, Pastor, Imago Dei Church, Raleigh, North Carolina

"For many of us, our twenties bring a swirl of change. Jobs, cities, relationships and ambitions all change. It's little wonder that such an overwhelming decade rakes up disappointment, rootlessness and questions of just where we fit in. Rachel empathetically shares how looking to Jesus comforts us and frees us to make the most of these years of flux."

PETER DRAY, Head of Creative Evangelism, UCCF

"Fantastic at demonstrating the relevance of the Bible to the 'quarter-life crisis', Rachel Jones widens our vision and gives us an eternal perspective."

JAGO WYNNE, Rector, Holy Trinity Clapham, London

"Rachel deftly articulates the discontent many feel when they find life as an adult hasn't turned out the way they expect, and she applies the Bible to that struggle. I am eager to use this book with those about to graduate."

RACHEL SLOAN, Women's Ministry Coordinator, Charlotte Chapel, Edinburgh

"Life in young adulthood can seem disorienting—this book gets how that feels, and helps you find your feet and walk with confidence. And for anyone who, like me, is well beyond young adulthood, Rachel helps you get inside how it feels to be a millennial or Gen-Z-er—to understand the tensions, hopes and fears, and how Christianity speaks to them."

RICO TICE, Senior Minister, All Souls Langham Place, London; Founder, Christianity Explored

"Honest, wise, practical and biblical. Rachel brings the gospel to bear in a humorous and sensitive way that will both challenge and encourage anyone who is discontent or disillusioned."

REUBEN HUNTER, Lead Pastor, Trinity West, London

"Rachel Jones is the friend who just gets you. In Is This It?, she covers profoundly deep and impactful issues for twentysomethings with relatability, honesty, and a healthy dose of humor. This book will address some of your deepest longings, fears and insecurities while meeting you with a firehouse of gospel grace and practical insight. I wish everyone my age could read this book!"

JAQUELLE CROWE, Author, *This Changes Everything*; Founder, The Young Writer

"Rachel Jones can put timeless truth into very timely words. Her voice is both current and weighty. I can't recommend this book highly enough."

STEF LISTON, Pastor, Revelation Church, London; Spoken Word Artist

"In an age of Instagram comparisons and Fear Of Missing Out, Rachel does an amazing job of pointing the dissatisfied back to Jesus and the satisfying truth of the Scriptures."

JERRAD LOPES, Founder of DadTired.Com

"This is a witty, engaging book that not only describes some of the challenges of modern Western life but in a fresh way articulates how the gospel of Jesus Christ meets us in our deepest desires and needs."

PAUL REES, Lead Pastor, Charlotte Chapel, Edinburgh

"When it comes to this generation in the grip of the 'quarter-life crisis', too often cynics roll their eyes while others merely reinforce their blindspots. By contrast, this book engages brilliantly with compassion, clarity, wit and, most importantly, much-needed, Christ-centred, grace-filled truth. This book is a gem—read it, share it with others and realise the difference Jesus makes!"

PETE NICHOLAS, Senior Minister, Inspire London; Author, *Virtually Human*

"I totally love this book! It's witty, honest and painfully real—a gem. I laughed out loud; I cried; I felt like Rachel could see into my head and she understood. Better still, she showed me the difference Jesus makes to life's questions.This book is so packed full of wisdom, I'll have to buy in bulk as I know I'll keep giving it away!"

LINDA ALLCOCK, Globe Church, London

"Here's some smart, solid, durable and proven wisdom—the kind of wisdom that's getting harder to find. So my advice for 20-somethings who love Jesus is this: get it and read it."

JOEL VIRGO, Senior Pastor, Emmanuel Church, Brighton, UK

# CONTENTS

# 31 REASONS YOU MIGHT NEED THIS BOOK

True or false? Score 1 point for every true answer.

1. You frequently find yourself asking, "What should I do with my life?"

2. Watching sitcoms from your adolescence on Netflix makes everything feel better.

3. You still keep loads of stuff in the house you grew up in.

4. You still keep loads of stuff in the house you grew up in because you still live there.

5. You wonder whether you've really got any friends anymore.

6. You feel out of place at church because everyone else seems to have kids, a perm or a teddy bear (because they're either a parent, a pensioner or four years old).

7. You dread family occasions because relatives will ask you what you're doing with your life.

8. Life was definitely better when you were a teenager.

9. You suspect that quitting everything and going travelling might just solve all your problems.

10. Social media leaves you with the miserable suspicion that most of your friends have more fun/a better relationship/more money/a better house/more friends than you do (1 point for each).

11. You've ended up in a job that has absolutely nothing to do with what you dreamed of doing when you were six (or eleven, or sixteen).

12. You don't know how to do grown-up things like defrosting a freezer or paying your bills without looking it up on the internet or calling a real adult.

13. You suspect your mother is a little bit sad that you're not married by now.

14. You're a bit sad that you're not married by now.

15. You are married and you're still a bit sad right now.

16. You're worried that everyone at work will find out that you're secretly terrible at it.

17. "Buy a house? WITH WHAT MONEY?"

18. You worry that you've got God's plan for your life wrong.

19. You worry that God's got his plan for your life wrong.

20. Looking closely in the mirror is an increasingly distressing experience.

21. You'd really like a job that you'd find more fulfilling... but you've got no idea what that would be.

22. You sometimes quietly wonder if you should give up on God.

23. You're just... a bit bored of life.

24. The way you wander aimlessly around Aldi or Walmart wondering what to have for dinner is a metaphor for your complete inability to make decisions. About anything.

25. Everyone else seems to be having babies, and you wonder how you got to this stage of life so quickly.

26. You didn't expect that being an adult would involve this much life admin.

27. Your back hurts.

28. Your bank account is like a black hole: no matter how much you earn, or how little you spend, there's never much left at the end of the month.

29. You catch yourself talking about the pros and cons of various household appliances with your friends and then saying, "WHEN DID WE GET THIS OLD?"

30. You find yourself asking, "Is this it?"

31. You're a parent to someone who would answer "true" to a lot of those questions, and you thought they'd have grown up by now—and you're not sure quite where things got stuck. (Add 5 points.)

## 20+ POINTS: YOU REALLY NEED THIS BOOK

You've reached the age that you thought you'd have life figured out by—and you're disappointed to find that you don't. Welcome to the club. This book is aimed right at you.

## 10-20 POINTS: YOU NEED THIS BOOK

You're doing an OK job at keeping it together as a fully-functioning grown-up. Some days you even do your own laundry and eat the recommended number of fruit and vegetable portions. Other days you lie in your bed with your duvet over your head when the alarm goes, asking "Why?" You need to read this book.

## 1-9 POINTS: YOU KIND OF NEED THIS BOOK

Well, OK, you seem to be more or less keeping it together—but now you've got this far you might as well carry on reading. Or maybe you're a student and you still have most of this ahead of you. In which case, read this book to prepare you for the day you find yourself wailing down the phone to an unsuspecting friend or relative, "WHAT AM I MEANT TO BE DOING WITH MY LIFE?"

## WHEN DID BEING GROWN-UP GET THIS HARD?

"Why did no one ever warn me that being an adult was going to be this... *difficult*?"

I was 24 years old, I was sitting on my bed, and I was feeling thoroughly sorry for myself.

It's not that life had fallen apart—it was more that it hadn't quite come together.

On one level, things looked OK. My job was secure, my rent was cheap and church life was busy.

And yet... I was desperately bored at work, secretly lonely at church—and don't even get me started on how weird my housemates were.

Nothing was *really wrong*, but none of it felt *quite right*. Whatever I had imagined adult life would be like, it wasn't this. I couldn't help but ask myself, "Is this it?"

It turns out that my experience was so unoriginal that there's even a name for it: the Quarter-Life Crisis. It can strike at pretty much any time in our 20s or early 30s. The networking website LinkedIn found that 75% of us report having one.

Unlike its older brother, the Midlife Crisis, the Quarter-Life Crisis has nothing to do with buying an expensive sports car (because, let's face it, we don't have that kind of money). Instead, it's that dawning realisation that you've reached the age by which you had always assumed that you'd have got it all (or at least some of it) figured out, only to find that you haven't at all. You're still incompetent at doing all the things that grown-ups are meant to be able to do—like keeping a house-plant alive, or topping up the rinse-aid in a dishwasher, or eating five portions of fruit and vegetables a day. And worse, you're overwhelmed by all the feelings and decisions that grown-ups are meant to be able to deal with.

You feel a little bit lost, a little bit lonely, a little bit like you're looking for something, but you're not even sure what.

The Quarter-Life Crisis creeps up on birthdays and New Year's Eves, and it rears its head any time you see on social media that someone you went to school with has had a baby, got a promotion, or simply had the audacity to look happy in a photo. It's that desire to change something about your life, but being overwhelmed by the options. It's the uneasy feeling that comes when you take stock of everything around you—the people, the places and the relentless routines of work and washing up—and find yourself asking, "Is this it?"

When I hit my personal "Is this it?" moment, and started to talk to my friends about how I was feeling, I discovered that they were having their own Quarter-Life Crisis too. One friend told me about how he was resigned to hating his job for ever.

Another said he was worried he'd made the wrong choices and got in the way of God's plan for his life. A third described how she had always imagined she'd be married with kids by the time she was 30, and how that was looking increasingly unlikely: "I feel like I'm grieving something I never had".

"Well," said a friend with a particularly dry sense of humour, "I think the Quarter-Life Crisis is when you've been out of education for a while and you start to realise that this is for ever. The next big life event is retiring or dying."

## THE MEASURE OF ADULTING RIGHT

So what on earth is wrong with us all? Maybe you're a bit older than the typical QLC-sufferer, and you'd like nothing more than to shake me by the shoulders and give me a reality check. Maybe you have identified the problem: I'm a self-absorbed 20-something who needs to just grow up and snap out of it.

And believe me, I'd love to.

First, because I know that there are Bigger Problems in the world than these. After all, if I'm feeling crippled by indecision about what to do with my life, that's because I'm privileged enough to have choices at all. Maybe you know what it feels like to have those kinds of Bigger Problems. Maybe adult life for you has so far been marked by bereavement, depression or chronic ill-health. Perhaps you're living with scars inflicted by someone else, or under the weight of a mistake you made years ago.

Second—and more importantly—because I know that the Christian life is not meant to feel like this. The Bible doesn't use the phrase "Quarter-Life Crisis", but it does use the word "trials". And this is what it says about them:

12

*Consider it pure joy, my brothers and sisters, whenever you face trials of many kinds, because you know that the testing of your faith produces perseverance. Let perseverance finish its work so that you may be mature and complete, not lacking anything. (James 1 v 2-4)*

People my parents' age tend to think that my generation just needs to grow up. God thinks something different: that we need to grow like Jesus.

These verses (and, for that matter, this book) are talking to people who are Christians—people who recognise who Jesus is and why that matters, and who try to live their lives in a way that honours him as King (and yet still enjoy his forgiveness when they mess that up). And being a Christian ought to turn our expectations of adulting on their head. If we're following Christ, life's big adventure is not climbing the career ladder or meeting milestones—it's about becoming "mature and complete" in our faith. So the measure of whether we're adulting right is not whether we've got our own place with a pet, but whether our character looks like Christ's.

That's what "maturity" means—becoming like Jesus, the most courageous, compassionate, convictional, kind grown-up of all time. How do we grow into that maturity? Through trials. What I love about this verse in James is that there isn't any difficult season that isn't covered by that catch-all phrase, "trials of many kinds". There isn't any problem that is too small to count—God sees it all, cares about it all, and wants to use it all. It's all these things that put our faith to the test and turn it into something tougher, wiser and more beautiful.

It's this truth that means that facing up to the question "Is this it?" can be "pure joy" too—even in the moments when we're sitting on our beds feeling sorry for ourselves. The indecision, the self-doubt, the rootlessness and the discontent can all be considered 100% pure joy—because they're an opportunity to appreciate more fully what Jesus gives, and to understand more clearly where real life is found.

Which sounds great.

The trouble is, I don't believe it.

Or at least, I don't really believe it—not in a way that grips my heart and my head and eclipses all the other things I secretly long for.

But I want to believe it—I want to taste that "pure joy" James talks about. Hence this book. I'm talking to myself really, but you're more than welcome to listen in. I'll warn you now that some of this may not be new to you—but sometimes, when we can't see the wood for the trees, we just need reminding of what we already know all over again. So over the next twelve chapters, we'll look at some of the challenges and emotions that grown-up life brings. You can read them in any order, depending on what you're feeling like. By the end of this book, it's my hope that you'll be that little bit closer not to being a proper grown-up, but to being "mature and complete" in Christ. Because persevering in following Jesus offers us something truer and better than chasing anything else in our 20s and 30s can.

Is this it?

No, it's not. There's more to this life, and there's more than this life.

Trust me. Or rather, trust Jesus. Everything is going to be OK.

# 1. DISSATISFIED

## HAS EVERYONE ELSE GOT IT BETTER THAN ME?

My old schoolfriend Amy really loves animals—so much so that she doesn't eat them.

So when she went to work in New Zealand for a year, the one thing she wanted was to see whales in the wild. She was living on the coast, in a bay that was famous for its whale appearances. She'd heard that occasionally they would even come and play among the swimmers who took an early-morning dip in the ocean.

Amy spent twelve months in New Zealand—and never saw a single whale.

Sometimes she'd see reports on local TV about sightings in the bay while she was at the office—but by the time she'd dashed down there, all the whales had gone. She spent hundreds of dollars and countless weekends on boat trips. She saw plenty of dolphins, but they weren't what she was there to see. It felt like they were mocking her with their pointy-toothed grins. She spent over a year living in the best place to see whales, but she didn't catch so much as a fin.

Rachel Jones

On her return home, we caught up over dinner, and we laughed as she recounted her futile whale-watching efforts. But later in the evening, she went on to tell me about the less funny side of her year abroad. When I told her I was writing this book and asked if she'd ever had a Quarter-Life Crisis, she replied:

"Oh, mine was probably New Zealand."

"What, you mean the fact that you went?"

"No..." she said, "the way that I dealt with it." She told me about the tearful phone calls home, the crisis of confidence in her relationship, and the way she quit a succession of jobs on impulse for reasons she couldn't quite explain.

I smiled ruefully. "Maybe your search for the whales was really all a metaphor for your search for..."

She shrugged: "Life satisfaction."

We're not all searching for whales—but we are all searching for *that*.

## EVERYONE ELSE HAS FOUND YOUR WHALES

We all spend our lives longing for and looking for something— something that will make us properly happy. We spend money in the pursuit of satisfaction, stockpiling it in the bank or splurging it on exotic trips. We spend time looking for satisfaction—investing our efforts in the relationships or the careers or the experiences we think will satisfy. But we always seem to just miss out. Contentment proves elusive—we never quite arrive at the state of "satisfied". And while most of us are not even sure what exactly it is that will make us happy, we're certain that we just saw a flash of its tail disappearing around the corner of the bay. So we keep looking.

I think that it's *this* feeling that perhaps most gets to the heart of the angst described on this book's cover. "I guess the emotion at the core of my mid-20s is longing," reflected another friend. "Longing for what I thought I'd have by now, and what other people have already."

Does that ring true for you right now? What do you long for?

What's that one thing which seems just out of your reach—but that you know, if you could just wrap your fingers around it, would make you feel satisfied?

Most people read that kind of question, and then cruise straight on to the next paragraph. But seriously, stop. Don't look down the page. Look up, and think about the question. Because I've never met anyone who didn't have that one thing, but I've met plenty who weren't sure what their one thing actually was.

Part of our dissatisfaction problem is that as we look at our screens, it seems that everyone else is waist-deep in the ocean, merrily frolicking with the whales of joy. It's ironic that while Amy was crying in an apartment in New Zealand, I was in an office on a nondescript business park back home, looking at her smiling photos and wishing that I could leave it all behind and head off for an adventure Down Under too. While every generation has been engaged in the pursuit of happiness since at least 1787 (when, my non-American friends, the right to do so was enshrined in the US Constitution), never before have we been able to keep up with how other people are doing on the quest quite like we can today.

Ours is the first generation in whose lives social media played a huge part during adolescence—there's reason to believe it has actually affected the way our brains have developed. And

"READ THE NEWSPAPER COLUMNS, AND YOU'LL QUICKLY GET THIS IDEA THAT OUR GENERATION IS ENTITLED AND DELUSIONAL."

#ISTHISIT

research shows that it's making us miserable. A study by the *Harvard Business Review* found that *even "liking" someone else's post* "significantly predicted a subsequent reduction in self-reported physical health, mental health, and life satisfaction". We don't "like" it at all. We resent it. Discontentment has an even uglier cousin called envy.

It's not just comparing ourselves with what *other* people have that makes us dissatisfied—we also compare ourselves with what we think *we* should have, or be. Tim Urban, of the website Wait But Why, makes the point that our generation has wildly optimistic expectations. We don't just want life to be like a lush green lawn, or even a lush green lawn with flowers. No—we want unicorns. In a sense, this isn't our fault. We've been raised to think that we're special and that life owes us shiny unicorns, and that we can expect them to turn up almost as soon as we start out on our adventure into adulthood. So when our work or our relationships or our church or life in general doesn't feel like shiny unicorns—when it feels, well, normal—we're unhappy. So we go looking somewhere else.

Or at least, that's what we're told—read the newspaper columns, and you'll quickly get this idea that our generation is entitled and delusional. Now, that assessment might be true of you, or at least partly true—or it might not be at all. Generational stereotypes are just that—stereotypes. In fact, before we continue, I think a couple of caveats are necessary.

First, you might be facing something really tough at the moment. Nothing you're about to read is intended to negate your pain. It's not wrong to want your circumstances to change, or to pray for God to change them. The aim of this chapter is not to help us like every circumstance, but to be content in the midst of every circumstance. There's a difference.

Second, it's not wrong to desire good things. It's OK to want to be married, or to desire a fulfilling job (or just *a* job), or to long to see justice done in your community. In fact, it's good to want these things. The issue comes when we start pointing the finger of blame—at others, at ourselves and at God. If we start to grumble against God, and accuse him in our hearts of withholding good things from us, we make out that he is an unloving Father who doesn't have our best interests at heart. That's when we have a problem.

And if you're anything like me, you do have a problem. You've been looking for the whales of satisfaction for a few years as an adult now, but you're no closer to finding them. Dissatisfaction turns the edges of your blue sky grey or eclipses the sun altogether. There's a sense of lack in an area of your life that you just can't fill. And you wish you didn't feel like this, because you know it's an unhappy and unhelpful and unfruitful way to live. But you do.

One man who had been on a (metaphorical) whale watch was the apostle Paul. And he'd found them. In his letter to the Philippian church he declared:

> *I have learned to be content whatever the circumstances. I know what it is to be in need, and I know what it is to have plenty. I have learned the secret of being content in any and every situation. (Philippians 4 v 11-12)*

I don't think Paul's trying to be smug. He's wanting to encourage us, in two ways. First, contentment is not automatic or easy. It has to be "learned", even if you're a top-apostle-come-evangelist-come-theologian like Paul was. But second, it is possible to learn. If you want to be content, know that you can be content—you've just got to learn.

But how? Well, like anything we learn, practice is better than theory. It requires some effort and a bit of advice from someone wiser (God, not me). So consider this chapter your guidebook to the art of whale-watching. First tip coming straight up...

## GET YOUR PERSPECTIVE RIGHT

If you've ever tried looking down the wrong end of a pair of binoculars, you'll know that instead of making things look bigger and closer, it makes them look smaller and further away.

Dissatisfaction starts when we look at the wrong things through the wrong end of the binoculars. We look at our earthly circumstances through the small end, so that they loom large in our vision. But we look at eternal things through the big end—so that they seem small, insignificant and far away. Yet in reality eternity is none of those things. It's big, it's important, and it's soon.

That's the lesson Asaph says he's learned in Psalm 73. This is a guy who sounds like he might have spent too much time scrolling on Instagram. And what did he feel? Jealous.

> *But as for me, my feet had almost slipped;*
> *I had nearly lost my foothold.*
> *For **I envied the arrogant when I saw the prosperity of the***
> ***wicked**. (Psalm 73 v 2-3, my emphasis)*

Here the "wicked" are not people who are particularly bad, but people who think either that God's not real or that he's not worth listening to. Yet that doesn't seem to be holding them back. These people are prosperous—they've got the clothes and the car and the house. They don't struggle with ill-health or feeling ugly—"their bodies are healthy and strong" (v 4). "They are free from common human burdens" (v 5)—no broken hearts, or lonely weekends, or threat of redundancy, or aging grandparents that they worry about. "They are not plagued by human ills" (v 5)—no anxiety or depression or anything else hard.

It looks like they've got it all together. These people are confident go-getters (v 6). They can talk their way into everything (v 9). They're in a position of influence (v 10). And they're not weighed down by any religious baggage: "How would God know? Does the Most High know anything?" they ask themselves (v 11). No one's making them get up early on a Sunday morning to do crowd control on a bunch of unruly Sunday-school kids. No one's making them give their money away, or talk to awkward people over lukewarm coffee. There are no rules to follow, no people to please—they can do as they want. They are "always free of care, [and] they go on amassing wealth" (v 12).

And when Asaph looks at what he has, and looks at what they have, he wants the latter:

> *Surely in vain I have kept my heart pure and have washed*
> *my hands in innocence.*
> *All day long I have been afflicted, and every morning brings*
> *new punishments. (v 13-14)*

And maybe as you look around, that's what you feel too. You secretly wonder whether you're really any better off or more fulfilled than your friends who don't bother with God. Maybe you secretly wonder why God has given some of your friends who *do* bother with him so much more than he's given you. You know this Christian stuff is meant to make you happy, but it's not really working. Instead you feel "afflicted"—worn down, let down and under pressure. You wish you had what other people had. Are you wasting your time with Jesus?

"No," says Asaph. And here's what changed his perspective:

*When I tried to understand all this, it troubled me deeply*
*till I entered the sanctuary of God; then I understood their*
*final destiny. (v 16-17)*

Asaph comes before God and has his binoculars on eternity turned the right way round. One day the wicked will be "cast ... down", "destroyed" and "swept away by terrors" (v 18-19). They will be "like a dream when one awakes"—barely remembered (v 20). Even the most vivid dreams, which fill your mind with colour and emotion at night, suddenly become inconsequential in the light of reality.

And this day of reckoning for those who don't bother about God is not far off. It is soon. We don't know when exactly it will come, but it will happen "suddenly" (v 19). When I envy my friends who are not Christians, I am being short-sighted. They might have everything; but God says they have nothing they can keep.

And once he's holding the binoculars on eternity the right way round, Asaph has fresh eyes to see what he does have:

*Yet I am always with you; you hold me by my right hand.*
*You guide me with your counsel, and afterwards you will*
*take me into glory.*
*Whom have I in heaven but you?*
*And earth has nothing I desire besides you.*
*My flesh and my heart may fail, but God is the strength of*
*my heart and my portion for ever. (v 23-26)*

The wicked are going to lose the stuff and the status pretty soon, but Asaph has something that will last "for ever": a relationship with God that goes from now into "glory" (v 24). God holds Asaph's hand with all the undivided attention, intimacy and security of a loving parent with a young child. He gives him counsel with all the wisdom and trustworthiness of an experienced mentor.

And more than anything, God satisfies. He's Asaph's "portion"—like a wholesome, hearty meal that fills you up, rather than snacks that give you a sugar hit but leave your teeth feeling fuzzy.

Asaph realises that everything the earth offers pales in comparison to this: "Whom have I in heaven but you?"

And that's the question you have to ask yourself too. Why chase whales that don't last, and won't ultimately satisfy, when you have something that will? Would you really trade your salvation for a skinnier figure or two weeks in St Lucia?

I love Asaph's honesty. He shows us that when we're feeling dissatisfied, we can be honest about that with God. We can tell him what it is we're longing for, and why we're tempted to think that the way life has panned out is unfair. But like Asaph, we can't stop there. We need to come to God and acknowledge that...

> When my heart was grieved and my spirit embittered, I was senseless and ignorant; I was a brute beast before you.
>
> (v 21-22)

Living our lives under a cloud of dissatisfaction isn't just miserable—it's sinful. It makes a mockery of what God has given us: a relationship with him. He is a good Father who gives us only good things. Dissatisfaction turns us into brute beasts. Cows in the field can't enjoy a relationship with God—they're animals! And when our minds are controlled by our desires, that's what we're like.

Maybe, right now, you need to ask God to turn your binoculars round.

## KNOW WHAT YOU'RE LOOKING AT

As any naturalist will tell you, you've got to know what you're looking at and what you're looking for. Otherwise you'll go charging across the ocean to catch the whale of satisfaction, only to discover that the splash of grey you saw was merely a rock sticking out of the surf (which is disappointing), or a shark (which is dangerous).

So how do we identify what will truly satisfy? Earlier we read that Paul had "learned the secret of being content". *Go on then, Paul,* you might think to yourself, *let us all in on it.*

Well, he actually already did, back in chapter one of his letter: "To live is Christ and to die is gain" (Philippians 1 v 21). Paul is satisfied because, live or die, he has what satisfies—or, rather, he has who satisfies. He has Christ. "To live is Christ and to die is gain" is a win-win equation—there is absolutely no way Paul can lose out. Live or die, Paul believes he's hit the jackpot.

I wish I shared his confidence. But the truth is, I don't. And my discontentment comes when I lose sight of either side of the "to live is Christ and to die is gain" equation.

Contentment is found in living a life that can be summed up in one word: Christ. Real, satisfying life is to be found in doing it with him—"to live is Christ". Whenever that kind of existence doesn't sound particularly attractive, it means I've lost sight of who Christ is, and therefore of what life with him is like.

To live is Christ—and Christ is compassion. When he sees a widow whose only son is being carried in the hearse to the graveyard, he doesn't walk on, sad but busy. His heart goes out to her, he stops, and he helps.

To live is Christ—and Christ is humble. When his disciples' feet need washing before a meal, he doesn't wave over the waiter on the minimum wage. He wraps a towel around his waist, gets on his knees, takes those mud- (and worse-)caked feet in his hands and washes them clean.

To live is Christ—and Christ is quick-witted. Whenever the Pharisees ask him trick questions, he is not left umming and ahhing as he desperately tries to think up a response. He turns the conversation on its head, speaks searing truth and leaves his opponents floundering.

To live is Christ—and Christ is gentle. When parents bring their kids to Jesus for a blessing, and the disciples shoo them away because they assume their master doesn't have time for babies, Jesus tells them they're wrong. He's got all the time in the world for the lowly and unimportant.

To live is Christ—and Christ is just. When he sees cheats making a quick buck off people's desire to worship, by selling animals for sacrificing in the temple at inflated prices, he doesn't just sigh and shake his head. He doesn't write an angry letter to the local newspaper or organise an online petition. He overturns the tables and chases the cheats out.

To live is Christ—and Christ sees people. When a blind beggar is calling out to him from the side of the road, Jesus sees a man, not a problem. He won't let other people tell this guy to be quiet. He doesn't toss him a few coins to shut him up or satisfy his own conscience, and then keep walking. He stops. He asks. He listens. He heals.

To live is Christ—and Christ is truth. He doesn't fudge the hard facts to preserve his popularity. He tells people what they need to hear. His sermons aren't boring. People are astonished by his teaching, saying, "No one ever spoke the way this man does" (John 7 v 46).

To live is Christ—and Christ loves. After all that, "having loved his own who were in the world, he loved them to the end" (13 v 1). He went all the way. He gave all that he had. He allowed those beautiful hands—hands that raised the dead, and turned tables, and hugged children, and washed feet—to be torn apart by nails. Why? Because he loves you. His hands are scarred so that yours—hands that grasp more, and push aside, and point blame, and clench in anger—can shake hands with his in heaven. He loved you to the end—all the way to the cross.

To live is Christ—*this* Christ. This is the One who lives *in us* by his Spirit. This is the One who controls our every breath. This is the One we know. This is the One we live for. This is the One we praise. This is the One we labour for. And "living Christ" satisfies.

Jesus is not like a whale that seems to be playing hard to get. He's not beyond our reach. He's not hiding around the corner. He's not waiting for us to pull our socks up and try a little harder. We already have him. And Christian, he is wonderful.

And yet, for Paul, there's a sense that there is something better ahead. That's why the second half of his equation is "to die is gain"—because when we depart from this body, those who are in Christ now will be with Christ then, "which is better by far" (Philippians 1 v 23). Those beautiful hands will take our own and welcome us home. "Living Christ" now is real. But living with Christ then will somehow be even *more* real.

Often, we try to solve our dissatisfaction by looking at what we don't have and trying to gain it. Unhappily single? Try online dating. Bored at work? Look for a new job. Don't like the way you look? There's a beauty treatment or a protein supplement for that.

But there's a better gain on the other side of the grave.

My dissatisfaction is worse when I'm not confident that to die is gain. It's why I hedge my bets and aim to enjoy as much as I can now, packing in the experiences and the milestones and the accolades—trying to gain, gain, gain what I can, while I can. And when I don't or can't gain what I long for, I'm discontent, because I fear I'm missing out.

But Paul says it's impossible to miss out. We're locked into a guaranteed win-win equation. To live is Christ, and to die is gain.

## HUNT FOR WHAT MATTERS

You might think that by this stage I've stretched the whale metaphor a little too far. And you'd probably be right. But Jesus himself was a big fan of an extended metaphor (or, as he liked to call it, a parable). While he didn't talk about people looking for whales, he did tell a story about a man looking for something else:

> *The kingdom of heaven is like a merchant looking for fine pearls. When he found one of great value, he went away and sold everything he had and bought it. (Matthew 13 v 45-46)*

This merchant is something of a pearl connoisseur. He knows his freshwater pearls from his South Sea pearls. When you go out for dinner with him, he becomes animated as he tells you about the latest development in pearl technology. Pearls are more than a job for him; they're a passion. He's got hundreds in his house, on display on the mantelpiece, and carefully stored in cases and trunks. They're meticulously categorised and lovingly polished.

And yet one day, he finds a pearl that's worth more than all of that. It's so valuable, and so beautiful, that it's worth sacrificing his whole collection for. It's even worth selling the dining-room table and the kitchen sink for.

Suddenly, the search that used to consume him doesn't matter so much. It doesn't matter that he can't hold on to all that other stuff. He can't, even if he wanted to—he's got his hands full with this new pearl. It's so big, so valuable and so mesmerisingly beautiful that he doesn't have eyes for anything else.

That's what knowing Jesus as King, and becoming part of his kingdom, is like—finding a pearl that is more valuable than anything else.

I wish I was like that merchant. But more often I want to treat Jesus as one pearl among many. I want to add him to my collection on the mantelpiece, alongside the holiday photos, the amazing job, the picture-perfect family, and cut-outs of the five-star reviews for this book. Sure, I want Jesus. But I want this other stuff too.

But Jesus is saying that it doesn't work like that. He's so valuable that he costs everything. And the way to stop the looking—the way to stop that frantic search for something to satisfy, and that soul-sapping comparison with what everyone else has—is to drop everything and treasure this pearl. That's the secret of contentment.

Because you won't be satisfied by getting more. You'll only be satisfied by getting Jesus. And ironically, the way you "get" him is by loosening your grip on the other stuff: by letting it go rather than desperately trying to gather it all together.

So what have you got on the mantelpiece? What are you lovingly polishing? Or what are you holding space for, hoping you'll have it some day?

Let it go. Look at Jesus. And keep looking. Because he can satisfy—today, tomorrow, for ever.

# 2. PARALYSED
# (OR MAYBE INDECISION)
## WHAT SHOULD I DO WITH MY LIFE?

13 QUESTIONS THAT WILL PUSH YOU TO THE EDGE OF A BREAKDOWN:

1. Should I get a new job?

2. But what career would *really* suit me?

3. Would I be better off relocating to a different city?

4. Is now the right time to move house? To where?

5. Is it OK to move church?

6. Or should I quit my job and go travelling?

7. Or at least work abroad for a bit?

8. How do you tell if you're meant to "go into ministry"? (What does that even mean?)

9. Should I go (back) to university?

10. Should I be saving more money? Or maybe I'm meant to be giving more to church?

11. Should I go out with this person? / Are we ready to get married?

12. Should I just, like... settle?

13. Is the rest of my life really going to be like *this*?

## THE PROBLEM WITH TOO MANY OPTIONS

For nine months, I'd been feeling a vague yet persistent sense of unhappiness. Everything bored me. As I tried to work out why I felt like this, I put it down to my circumstances. I didn't especially like what I was doing, and I especially didn't like where I was living.

It was, I realised, time to take control—to make some big decisions and move my life on to the next stage.

So I looked at other jobs... but never applied. I looked at other houses... but never moved. Finally, after several months of feeling thoroughly fed up, I did something radical.

I auditioned to appear on a TV game show.

I knew I wanted something to change, but I wasn't sure what exactly it was, or how to change it. What if changing something made things worse? Turns out I wasn't trapped in my circumstances—I was trapped inside my head. And applying for a TV game show was easier than making a decision and taking a risk on something I actually cared about.

This is what Kevin DeYoung calls "tinkering" in his book *Just Do Something*. Some of us tinker with little things: sports and hobbies and boxsets on Netflix. Others of us tinker with bigger things: a string of jobs we never quite settle in, or a string of hearts we never quite commit to.

I tinker quite happily... until someone I know hits a major milestone—promotion, house, marriage, baby—and then I start to panic that I should be doing those things too. Or someone I don't see very often will say, "So, still working at the book place then?" and I'll give a sheepish smile and say, "Yeah, still there", while inwardly wanting to scream.

It's easy to tinker enough to fill the hours of your existence. But pretty soon we realise that tinkering doesn't actually make life go anywhere. We find ourselves feeling like Ian:

> *"Ian told me his twentysomething years were like being in the middle of the ocean, like this vast, unmarked body of water. He couldn't see land in any direction, so he didn't know which way to go. He felt overwhelmed by the prospect that he could swim anywhere or do anything. He was equally paralyzed by the fact that he didn't know which of the anythings would work out. Tired and hopeless at age twenty-five, he said he was treading water to stay alive."*
> (Meg Jay, The Defining Decade, page 32)

This is the paralysis of adulting. We feel unable to make decisions, because there are so many paths to choose from, and we're not sure where we're aiming to get to. And we can't figure that out because we don't know what it is that will make us feel happy and fulfilled. So we keep our options open—even as they overwhelm us—so that we don't miss out or get it wrong. And in doing so, we never go anywhere. Or we try to go everywhere.

What Ian needed—and what we all need—was a plan, a passion and a purpose.

And the good news is: we have them.

# THE PLAN

Most of us hate the idea that we're drifting from day to day, week to week, year to year, with no real sense of direction. We want life to go somewhere. But where? Perhaps you have always envied those people with a Life Plan—you know, those rare (and sometimes kinda smug) individuals who know where they want their life to go, and are able to make it go there. Or maybe you *are* one of those people (without the smugness, I'm sure), and underneath you're desperately worried about keeping the Plan on track and whether the destination will be worth it.

This need to be going somewhere is hardwired into us. Part of what God made when he created the universe is the dimension of time itself. We're itching to feel like we're going somewhere because the world around us *is* going somewhere—the Creator has set his creation on a timeline from A to B. And we're going somewhere with it. The question is... where?

That's what Paul addresses in his letter to the Ephesians:

> *As for you, you were dead in your transgressions and sins, in which you used to live when you followed the ways of this world and of the ruler of the kingdom of the air, the spirit who is now at work in those who are disobedient. All of us also lived among them at one time, gratifying the cravings of our flesh and following its desires and thoughts. Like the rest, we were by nature deserving of wrath. But because of his great love for us, God, who is rich in mercy, made us alive with Christ even when we were dead in transgressions— it is by grace you have been saved. And God raised us up with Christ and seated us with him in the heavenly realms in Christ Jesus, in order that in the coming ages he might show the incomparable riches of his grace, expressed in his kindness to us in Christ Jesus. (Ephesians 2 v 1-7)*

"Well, what does *that* have to do with my decisions?" I hear you ask. Here's what.

Western culture tells me that my life is an exciting journey to an as-yet-undecided-but-probably-awesome destination. But the picture of my "journey" in this passage is much more unnerving. It's more like I've cut the brakes on my own car, and now I'm racing down a hill towards a certain—and painful—collision with God's righteous anger.

Why? Because I'm instinctively and deliberately rebelling against the God who made me; I'm bent on serving my own interests and shutting out his; I'm spiritually dead. It sounds stark, but the Bible insists that it's true. And if I'm heading for this cosmic car crash, then no plan or passion or string of inspired decisions along the journey is ultimately going to make much difference to the end-point.

But there's a but. "But because of his great love for us, God, who is rich in mercy, made us alive with Christ even when we were dead in transgressions—it is by grace you have been saved."

If you're a Christian, it is because God has reached down and intervened to stop the car crash, "and [he has] raised us up with Christ and seated us with him in the heavenly realms in Christ Jesus" (v 6). That's what happened the moment you heard and believed "the message of truth, the gospel of your salvation" (1 v 13). If you are following Christ then, by God's grace, you've already made the most important decision of your life. Compared to that one, the others are just details.

Becoming a Christian is like doing a commando roll out of your own hell-bound car and being bundled by God into the back of Christ's car instead—the Bible calls this being "united to him" by faith. Now it's the case that where he goes, you go. So just as Christ died and was raised, you've been brought to real spiritual life too.

This reality is both "now and not yet". God has already "seated us with [Christ] in the heavenly realms". You have real, resurrection-quality spiritual life right now. There's a seat at heaven's wedding banquet with your name on it already. You can enter the throne room for a private audience with the King of the universe any time you pray. But there's something more coming, too: "in the coming ages", when all Christ's people are gathered in to the party, we will at last together fully display the breathtaking scale of God's grace, and will at last be able to praise our Saviour face to face.

We're part of a story that is building to a climax where Jesus is glorified for ever. Your existence is not one of aimless drifting—you've got a destination. Where you'll be in 50 years' time is uncertain. Where you'll be in 500 years is not. This is not for maybe; this is for sure. So when you're surrounded by a set of "maybes" (*maybe I should do this, maybe I should move there, maybe I should go out with him*), look ahead to what *is* sure—and so, so exciting.

In this sense, life can't go "wrong". All the decisions, indecisions and curveballs you experience can never make it go wrong.

And maybe you need to hear that, right now. Maybe you were sure you'd found the right girl to marry... but then she broke things off. Or you were successfully "adulting"... but then ill-health hit and you had to move back in with your parents. Perhaps you and your spouse were both ready to start a family... but now you're staring in the face of infertility. Or you landed the job for which you'd been studying for years... but a few months later you were made redundant.

Our culture says that if we just work hard enough or believe in ourselves enough, we can make what we want to happen happen. But maybe you've learned the hard way that that's simply not true. There are some things that are outside of our control.

These verses remind us what kind of Person *is* in control: it is the God who has "great love for us" (v 4), who is "rich in mercy (v 4) and "grace" (v 7), all of which are shown most clearly and compellingly in his extraordinary "kindness to us in Christ Jesus" (v 7). He might not take you on quite the route that you would plan, but he has intervened to set you on course to the only destination worth heading to.

## THE PASSION

If our parents expect us to have a plan, then our friends expect us to have a passion. *Don't worry too much about making plans or hitting milestones,* the thinking goes. *Just do the things that make you happy.*

And if you're anything like me, this leaves you scratching your head: What is my passion? How do I find it? Am I happy enough yet? How will I tell?

When you're in your 20s or early 30s, there's a lot of pressure to "find yourself"—to discover the career or the relationship or the niche or the experience that will fulfil you. If you're not loving life, something is wrong and you need to change it. Buzzfeed, that great guru of our age, sums it up: "Ultimately, your career of choice should make you come alive. And if that's not happening, it's OK to yearn for more" (*15 Important Reminders For Everyone Going Through A Quarter-Life Crisis,* December 19, 2014).

There's nothing wrong with wanting to feel alive—it really is "OK to yearn for more". But you'll always be disappointed if you don't look in the right place for that feeling; you can only be made alive *"with Christ"* (v 5).

Grasp this, and you'll see that the gospel of Jesus Christ is the only thing worth being truly passionate about. My reason for living is not to bristle with passion at what is, and always will be, a fairly mediocre existence (even if I do win big on that game show, or sell a million copies of this book). My reason for living is to give Christ all the kudos—showing how glorious and gracious and loving and kind he is—as I live as one of his people. If I had a heart that truly grasped this, I wouldn't get so swept up in the trivial bits of life that I'm tinkering with. I wouldn't feel the need to search for fulfilment—mixing and matching the puzzle pieces of life, looking for a combination that "clicks"—because I would be busy enjoying the reality that Christ has already sought me out and made me spiritually alive in him.

And I'd be freed from paralysis too. Life in Christ frees us to take risks. The Christian answer to the question "What if I do this thing and then it doesn't work out or I don't like it?" is, "Well, if you do, and then it doesn't or you don't, you'll still be alive with Christ". You'll still have the thing that makes life now worth living—as well as the ticket to the only future destination worth heading for.

Life may not always go the way you want. Decisions may not always work out the way you hoped. And that's OK. Because you know the destination, and you know the driver. It's Christ, and it's Christ. And that's worth getting excited about. Take the job; don't take the job. Go on the date; don't go on the date. Look for somewhere else to live; don't look for somewhere else

"LIFE MAY NOT ALWAYS
GO THE WAY YOU WANT.
AND THAT'S OK.
BECAUSE YOU KNOW THE
DESTINATION AND YOU
KNOW THE DRIVER."

#ISTHISIT

to live. But whatever else you do, do the only thing that can make you feel truly alive—do life with Christ.

## THE PURPOSE

God's plan and his passion give us a new purpose:

> *For it is by grace you have been saved, through faith—*
> *and this is not from yourselves, it is the gift of God—not*
> *by works, so that no one can boast. For we are God's*
> *handiwork, created in Christ Jesus to do good works, which*
> *God prepared in advance for us to do. (Ephesians 2 v 8-10)*

This is the purpose you were born (again) for: to do good works.

More than that, there are *specific* good works which God has "prepared in advance" for you to do. Just think about that for a moment: God—the author of this great cosmic plan to demonstrate his grace—has lined up good works specifically for you to do as part of that plan. Every good work we do demonstrates that we've been created anew "in Christ Jesus"—that we've been brought from death to life by a gracious God.

If we're not careful, though, this can quickly lead us down another existential hole. Instead of thinking, "What do I want to do with my life?" we might end up asking, "What does God want me to do with my life?"—and then have a hard time desperately trying to figure out exactly what his "plan" is. If he's prepared good works for me, are they in this city, or that other city? With a spouse, or staying single? What if I choose the wrong option?!

This way of thinking about "God's plan for your life" is guaranteed to give us a headache—and it's just not how he operates. It's not that God's holding the treasure map and we have to guess the route to the X that marks the spot. More often than not, it's only in hindsight that we can trace God's hand as we look back over the journey. The application of Ephesians 2 v 10—to "do good works, which God prepared in advance for us to do"—is not to do a specific set of good works that we have to locate, but to just "do good works" as they come into our path. As we do so, we can know that they're precisely the ones that God has planned. If we're doing good works, it's impossible to be doing the "wrong" ones.

God has prepared good works for you to do in the next 50 years. There are the big ones—perhaps a spouse for you to cherish, children for you to raise, parents for you to care for, vulnerable people for you to help, friends for you to call into his kingdom. There are solutions for you to dream up, and dreams for you to implement.

And God has prepared good works for you to do today. There are messes for you to tidy and meals for you to cook. There are church friends for you to encourage, and neighbours for you to pray for, and work to do diligently.

Some good works will be easy; others will be costly. Some will be fun; others will be painful. Some will take you years; others will be done with barely a moment's thought. But each one is prepared specifically for you by your Saviour. That is reason enough to get out of bed in the morning, on each and every morning the Lord gives you.

## HOW TO ACTUALLY, REALLY, MAKE A DECISION

All this means that we don't need to figure out the one specific God-ordained route through life. But we do need *a* route, right? And this is where a dose of common sense and wisdom helps us to move from indecision to action.

## 1. LIMIT YOUR OPTIONS

As a Christian, the first question always to ask is "Is this a 'good work'?" Put another way, is it sinful? So if you're considering going out with a non-Christian, the answer is "Don't". Likewise, if you're considering taking a job in a strip club,. the answer is "Don't". But most decisions are morally neutral. "Should I stay at this company or look for a new job?" Well, both of those options would probably involve doing good work. Trickier still is, "What kind of new job should I look for?" The endless opportunities can quickly feel overwhelming.

In *The Defining Decade,* Meg Jay writes about an experiment in how consumers make choices. In one instance, customers in a grocery store were offered six types of jam to sample for free. In another instance, there were 24 flavours to choose from. The bigger display generated more attention but fewer sales: only 3% of customers bought jam. But when choosing from only six flavours, 30% of customers did.

Here's the conclusion she draws:

> *"Twentysomethings hear they are standing in front*
> *of a boundless array of choices. Being told you can do*
> *anything or go anywhere is like ... standing in front of*
> *the twenty-four-flavour table. But I have yet to meet a*
> *twentysomething who has twenty-four viable options. ...*
> *You've spent more than two decades shaping who you are.*
> *You have experiences, interests, strengths, weaknesses,*
> *diplomas, hang-ups, priorities ... You're standing in front of*
> *six flavours of jam and you know something about whether*
> *you prefer kiwi or black cherry." (pages 35-36)*

(With a jam selection like that, she's definitely doing her shopping in a classier place than I am. But you get the point.)

If there's an area of life that's agonising you at the moment, what are the flavours of jam that you're standing in front of? What are the viable options? Write them down or talk them over with a Christian who knows you well. Make them specific.

## 2. CONSIDER YOUR MOTIVES

Next, think through your motives. What is it that's making you want to change (or not change)? What is attracting you to a particular option? Is it fear (of the unknown, of risk, of what someone will think of you, of being alone)? Is it pride? Is it material gain? Or is it a better motive—a desire to serve God with more of your time or gifts?

Motives are hard to figure out, because "the heart is deceitful above all things and beyond cure. Who can understand it?" (Jeremiah 17 v 9). It's why we constantly need to seek to cultivate wisdom through reading God's word—that's where we see clearly God's perfect standards as a yardstick against which to measure our own mixed motives.

It also means that prayer is an important element of making a decision. It's tempting to ask God to just tell us what he wants us to do: "Lord, give me a sign already. What should I do?" But that's playing into the treasure-map approach to God's will. It's better instead to pray like Paul prayed for the Philippians:

*[I pray] that your love may abound more and more in*
*knowledge and depth of insight, so that you may be able*
*to discern what is best and may be pure and blameless for*
*the day of Christ, filled with the fruit of righteousness that*
*comes through Jesus Christ. (Philippians 1 v 9-11)*

The Philippians must "discern what is best", and that discernment is built upon knowing God better and better. That suggests that a decision is something we ask God for help with and then think hard about, trusting that he's working within us rather than writing the answer in the sky.

Most of the time, our motives are a confusing mix of the good and the ugly—search hard enough and you'll almost always find elements of the latter. That's not a reason not to do something. But where your motives are almost all self-serving and not honourable, then that should probably be a red flag.

### 3. SEEK COUNSEL

Ask a few people—people who know you well, love Jesus a lot, and have more life experience—for their counsel. Listen carefully, and be prepared to change course as you think through what they say. Don't keep asking more and more people until someone gives you the answer you want.

This is where it is helpful to have limited your options; you're more likely to have a constructive conversation with someone that begins "I'm thinking of doing X or of doing Y. What do you think?" than simply wailing down the phone, "Dad, what should I *do* with my life?"

### 4. DO SOMETHING

With all that said and done, this last one's crucial: just make a decision.

If you decide "no", make it a "no". That doesn't mean you can't ever decide "yes" later down the line—sometimes it's wise to revisit the decision if your circumstances or character change with time. But what's not helpful is living in an ongoing state of paralysis, with a permanent sense of "Maybe..." hanging over your head. If you've decided it's best to stay in your job until the end of the year, stop looking at job websites. If you've decided you shouldn't marry the guy, break up with him. If you've decided you can't afford to go travelling next summer, stop scrolling travel hashtags on Instagram.

If it's a "yes", then do it. Figure out what the first step in getting there is, and then get on and do it.

As you do so, you can be excited and confident that these are good works that God has prepared for you.

Don't be paralysed by a fear of failing—by grace you're heading to heaven regardless, and you can't get off track.

Don't be paralysed by a fear of missing out on life—it's Christ who makes you alive, not anything else, and he'll be right there with you.

Don't be paralysed by a fear of failing to find your true purpose—as long as you're doing good works for his glory, you're doing what you were made for.

What should you do with your life? I think you're closer to knowing than you think.

# 3. ROOTLESS

## CAN I GO HOME NOW?

My mother had won, at last.

For several visits home, she had been begging could we please, please, please, sort through all the clutter in my childhood bedroom. (By "home" I mean my parents' house, where I grew up—not the rented room in a houseshare 250 miles away where I actually spend 330+ nights of the year.)

I'd managed to resist for a while. First, because time at home is for rest and relaxation—I don't want to spend it sorting through the dusty detritus of my adolescence. Second, because I harbour suspicions that my mother has designs to turn my room into something else: a guest bedroom, or a craft room, or a home gym. I'm sure that the cross trainer which has already appeared since I moved out is only the thin end of the wedge.

But on this trip home, my conscience got the better of me, and I finally agreed to a sort-out. As we emptied the cupboards, the contents went into four piles: things to throw away (old bank statements, used-up pens, broken gadgets), things to go to the charity shop (old clothes, tacky ornaments), things to take back to my actual house (important paperwork, spare batteries), and things to keep in my parents' house "Until I Am a Real Grown-Up with a Real Home of My Own".

This last pile was the biggest.

I looked at the stack of novels, artwork, homeware and photographs and sighed wistfully. There was no chance of it being resettled in a Real Home of My Own any time soon.

My mother looked at the pile and sighed sympathetically. Then back in the cupboard it went, until such time as I finally get my Real Home or my mother finally loses patience with it being in hers. Thankfully, so far she feels sorry for me.

## MISSING HOME

People of our generation in the UK are half as likely to own our own home by the age of thirty as those of our parents' generation were. 40% of us will still be renting when we hit the big 3-0. Saving for that elusive housing deposit is made difficult by rising rents—I'm fairly typical in handing around 45% of my take-home pay straight over to my landlord. And of course the real victims of the housing crisis are those living in temporary, unsuitable or overcrowded accommodation.

Not only is renting expensive; it's unstable. In the last four years, I've lived in four different houses, with a revolving cast of (sometimes peculiar) housemates. Americans will, on average, go through eleven relocations in their lifetime—the majority of them in their 20s. I was speaking to one friend about what had made the last year difficult for her. A company restructure had adversely affected her job, and her health hadn't been great, but it was moving house twice that had really taken it out of her. "I find moving... unsettling," she said. *Unsettling*. No wonder so many of us end up feeling unmoored.

To be honest, it's not a house I long for; it's home—which is why I still get homesick. I miss lounging on the sofa doing the quiz in the newspaper with my siblings. I miss my mother's lasagne. I miss friends who've known me since I was little. I miss the family pet rabbit. Perhaps that resonates with you— or perhaps you wish that you could miss those kinds of things, but your home life as a kid was messy and broken, and the homesick ache you feel now as an adult is the ache for something you never really had.

My problem (or rather, one of my problems) is that often when I go home, I find it's not quite what I was missing after all. As I'm writing this, it's almost Christmas, and I'm looking forward to what is one of the sweetest moments of my whole year. Not gathering round the table, or reliving childhood traditions, or joking around with my brothers, but driving home for Christmas while listening to Chris Rea's song "Driving Home for Christmas". Because driving home is often better than getting home. The anticipation—the ideal—is in some ways better than the reality.

In the reality of home, I find myself bickering with my brothers and criticising my parents. It turns out that my friends are busy, the lasagne is burned, and the childhood rabbit... well, he's long dead.

Maybe you're aware every day that home isn't what it used to be—because we're not just "Generation Rent"; we're also "the Boomerang Generation". In the US, as many as 40% of young adults live with their parents. In the UK, it's more than a quarter. Maybe that's you, and you hate it—you resent the limits on your freedoms, or your relationship with your family is strained, or worse. Even if you love the creature comforts, you're probably still hoping to move out some day.

I suspect, though, that wherever we're living—even if we're homeowners—we share a sense that life will get good once we're Somewhere Else. Where exactly Somewhere Else is will vary. It might be a house; or a bigger house with another bedroom; or another city or country.

My longing for home isn't really about my mother's lasagne at all. What I'm looking for is a sense of warmth, permanence and rootedness. But it's always just around the corner.

## RADICAL ROOTLESSNESS

We normally think of this rootlessness as a problem that needs fixing—mainly by earning more, saving harder and buying bigger.

But what if being part of "Generation Rent" actually gave us a unique opportunity to live for Jesus more wholeheartedly?

They say that an Englishman's home is his castle—but in Western culture it's more likely that an Englishman's home is his idol (and that's probably true of an American's or an Australian's too). It's what people work for in the present and what they look to to guarantee their security in the future. It fills our TV screens, our magazines and our dreams.

Yet, like any idol, it never quite delivers what people want it to. Get a foot on the housing ladder, and it's not long before you start looking two rungs up at what other people have. Somewhere Else stubbornly refuses to become Right Here.

And if your church is anything like mine, homes are an idol in your church culture too. I think I spend more time listening to people talk about buying homes and renovating homes in that 15-minute slot at the end of a Sunday service than I do any other subject—including talking about Jesus.

Yet Jesus never called us to come after him and settle in a three-bed semi with off-road parking. No...

> *As they were walking along the road, a man said to him, "I will follow you wherever you go." Jesus replied, "Foxes have dens and birds have nests, but the Son of Man has nowhere to lay his head." (Luke 9 v 56-58)*

Jesus lived a life of radical rootlessness. He grew up in Nazareth, but once he started his three-year teaching ministry, he was officially of no fixed abode. In the Gospels, we see him roving across the Middle-Eastern countryside, preaching, healing and miracling. He's not just renting—he's sofa surfing.

Jesus wasn't having an existential crisis, or even a financial one. His radical rootlessness was all part of his mission to proclaim "the kingdom of God"—the good news that anyone can enjoy life with him, now and eternally, by repenting of their sin and believing in him (Mark 1 v 15). Subjects of this kingdom become "foreigners and exiles" in this world, as they follow their King down his road of radical rootlessness (1 Peter 2 v 11).

The King's road is a road with a destination: home. Jesus describes heaven as his "Father's house [with] many rooms ... And if I go and prepare a place for you, I will come back and take you to be with me that you also may be where I am" (John 14 v 2-3).

Which means that right now, you're driving home for Christmas—and the destination will not disappoint.

You're driving towards endless celebration and feasting, with a banquet that will put the best Christmas dinner in the shade. This home is safe and permanent—there'll be no rogue landlord or dodgy neighbours. It's where our family is—a multitude of perfected brothers and sisters to celebrate with.

Best of all, waiting eagerly at the door to welcome us in is Jesus himself. He's the One who knows us and loves us more deeply than we can imagine—the One who left his home in heaven, lived the life of a roaming preacher and died the death of a social outcast to bring us home. Now he's standing at heaven's door, ready to embrace us and say, "Welcome home".

It's not wrong to long for home—this rootless feeling can be genuinely painful. But when we feel that way, it's an opportunity to set our hearts not on a 40-year mortgage but on the home with Jesus that we were made for. If we feel as if we're floating through life with little to tether us down, we can rejoice that the swirl of the currents will eventually wash us up on eternity's shore. Home, at last.

## PASSING THROUGH

Remembering that we're driving home for heaven changes our expectations on the journey, too. The point behind Jesus' foxes-and-birds comment is that if we want to follow him home, it often means giving up our comfort on the way there. The priority now is to "go and proclaim the kingdom of God" (Luke 9 v 60).

This is wonderfully liberating. It means that it doesn't matter if you haven't bought a house. It doesn't matter if you never buy a house. You haven't failed at life. Being a citizen of the kingdom of God—and telling others about its King and showing others the love of its King—is what matters. And a flexible, no-strings-attached lifestyle brings certain advantages to that end. I know a guy who lives with his parents and earns a living doing bank shifts in hospitals, so that he can take his medical skills to mission hospitals around the world at short notice. Is he wasting his 20s? I don't think so.

I find this hugely challenging, too. Whether we're giving generously to church matters far more than whether we're banking money in our savings account. What does your bank account say about where your priorities lie? Sure, there's such a thing as financial prudence. But Jesus didn't talk much about it. Are you embracing radical rootlessness for the sake of Christ—ready to go where he wants and give what it takes to honour him? Is your mind set on proclaiming the gospel, or do you spend more time daydreaming about getting the keys to a house? Are your expectations for where and how you'll live pretty similar to those of the people you went to school with? Might it be that you've bought the world's lie that settling down is what's important? I know that, all too often, I have.

The last time I moved house, I felt a little sad as I packed my life into boxes. Seeing all my worldly possessions in the back of a van reminded me that there's not much to them. They looked kind of pathetic.

As part of the move, I threw a lot of stuff out (this time, without my mother having to nag me). As I went to put a stack of old wedding invites, cards and keepsakes into the paper recycling, I hesitated. But I made myself do it, reminding myself that I don't need to cling on to this stuff in an attempt to make myself feel at home. I'm just passing through. I've got a better home waiting.

## SETTLE DOWN ALREADY

Settling down is not the goal. Except that, in one very specific sense, it should be.

Just as heaven is described as God's house in the Bible, the church is described as God's household—an extension of that family gathering in eternity: "Consequently, you are no longer foreigners and strangers, but fellow citizens with God's people and also members of his household" (Ephesians 2 v 19). We often miss the power of the way the New Testament describes our relationship with other Christians. We're not neighbours, or even friends. We're family: "brothers and sisters".

The trouble is that when it comes to church, a lot of us would rather stay as "foreigners and strangers" who are just passing through. Some of our rootless wanderings in our 20s and 30s are a product of circumstances: they're down to the job market or our housing situation. But there's a danger that our sense of rootlessness is partly self-inflicted. We're longing for home, but at the same time, we don't really want to settle down.

A friend of mine recently confessed that the thought of marrying her boyfriend and living in her suburban town for the rest of her life made her feel suffocated. I could sense her rising panic as she talked about it.

When I accepted a different role at my company earlier this year and committed myself to it long-term, I felt a little suffocated too. The idea that I would still be here for the rest of my 20s—in this town, this job, this church—made me irrationally afraid. See, I'm longing for home, but I'm itching to leave. I want home, but I don't want home to be this. Not here, not yet, not now. Home is Somewhere Else. Somewhere better. Somewhere I'm not. (And in the meantime, I'll daydream about a delayed gap year travelling around South America.)

But I'm wrong. Home is where God's people are. That means that the right thing to do—and not only that, the most fulfilling thing to do—will be to invest here, rather than always wishing I was somewhere else. If I have my mind constantly set on "What's next?"—thinking that my current reality is just for now—I'm in danger of finding myself present in body but not in spirit. Sure, life might take me elsewhere eventually, but that time is not yet. Living life on hold is not helpful; instead, I need to let my church start to feel like home. So do you.

So put down some roots in church. You'll find your life is much healthier for it.

## HOW TO MAKE A CHURCH A HOME

Maybe you're desperate to feel rooted at your church, but you've been going along for a while and it still doesn't feel like home. It's awkward and uncomfortable—you don't really know people, and they don't really know you. God might have made you "one body" in Christ, but you feel like you're out on a limb.

If that's you, don't pull back: dig in. It's as we do church that we feel church—and that's just as much the case if it's the church we've been going to for two months, or if it's the church we've grown up in for 20 years.

In Romans 12 v 9, Paul says that our love for other believers within the church "must be sincere". How do we grow that kind of rooted, heartfelt, I'll-stick-by-you, you're-my-family, sincere kind of love?

As we read on, Paul gives us a few principles for how we start making God's household feel like a home.

### 1. GO

*Be devoted to one another in love. Honour one another above yourselves. (v 10)*

A big part of being devoted to one another is being devoted to meeting together: "... not giving up meeting together, as some are in the habit of doing, but encouraging one another" (Hebrews 10 v 25).

It's hard to love people if we don't know them, and it's impossible to know people if we don't see them. So if church isn't something you're in the habit of going to every week, can I encourage you to start? If you don't have a church you're regular at, pick one. Some of us find church really hard—but it is so worth persevering with. If that's you, there's a helpful book tip in the extra resources section on page 205.

Once you've found a church to be part of, go big to go home. Attend two services on a Sunday if you can, and you might find that church feels like home in half the time. Join a Bible-study group, and block out that evening in your diary. Have a "Sorry, I can't do Tuesdays" mentality when other invites crop up.

And protect your Sundays. I once counted up how many Sundays I had been away from my church over the previous six months and was surprised to find it was about 20%. They were decent reasons—time away with friends, a weekend to see my parents, a wedding—and I was often at a church wherever else I was. But it's not the same if it's not my church.

So look back through your calendar and do the math for yourself now. If we spend much of our time being somewhere else, and then wonder why we don't feel settled, it might be because we're not getting the balance right. Sometimes the right thing to do is to say no, or cut short a weekend away and make the extra effort required to get back in time to see our church family.

## 2. SERVE
*Never be lacking in zeal, but keep your spiritual fervour, serving the Lord. (Romans 12 v 11)*

"Some people see the church as a giant helicopter. They're scared to get too close in case they get sucked into the rotas," jokes the comedian Milton Jones.

Maybe you, too, are scared of the rotas (or rosters, if you're American—but then the joke doesn't work). Yes, church bureaucracy makes me groan inside too—but if you are not yet serving in some way at church, it's probably time you started. Sure, it might inconvenience your weekends away (see Point One). No, you probably didn't dream of spending a chunk of your weekend serving coffee, directing traffic or looking after other peoples' toddlers. And yes, it is possible to serve in ways that aren't quite so organised.

But let's be grown-ups. In a family, it's only little children who get everything done for them. Take washing up. When we are very little, our parents wash all the dishes. When we are a bit older, we help out because we're made to. But you can tell you're a real adult when you start offering to wash up for your parents because you want to—or, at least, because you know that you should want to. (If you haven't yet reached this final stage, take this as the main application of the chapter and stop reading.)

Well, it's time to be a grown-up when it comes to church. How that looks will be different depending on what's needed. Don't do the minimum to be socially acceptable—do the maximum you can (although be warned that there is such a thing as doing too much). The important measure is attitude—throw yourself into it. Serve "zealously". And as you do so, you might find the fervour on your spiritual thermometer increasing. You'll get to know people better as you serve them and serve alongside them. You'll begin to feel invested.

So make a point of asking someone in charge at your church how you can get more involved. They'll be delighted. Almost every rota/roster has a gap that could have your name in it.

## 3. WAIT

*Be joyful in hope, patient in affliction ... Rejoice with those who rejoice; mourn with those who mourn. (v 12, 15)*

So you've done Steps One and Two and are still not feeling it? Step Three is in some ways easier and in other ways much harder.

Just hang in there. Be patient.

I've been at my church for four years. There was an initial six-month honeymoon period when I was "new"—everyone was friendly, though everything was small talk. The next six months after that were harder—I figured that was normal. When the next six months were hard too, I reasoned that maybe the settling-in period was longer than I had anticipated. But when after two-and-a-half years relationships still felt mostly shallow and dissatisfying, I felt deeply discouraged.

But I've come to realise that real relationships take time... a lot of time. The university experience leaves some of us with misguided expectations about how long this takes. There's no miracle-growth formula for fast-tracking deep friendships— they grow as the seasons change around them. They grow as we rejoice together over life's victories, as we cling together to the gospel when there's little else to find hope in, and as we mourn together in the face of suffering and loss.

The thing is that most of us don't fit that much "life" into a couple of months, or even a couple of years. So hang in there, and keep your eyes open for signs that your relationships are growing: for the steady growth of a leaf, the sudden blossom of a flower, or—harder to see but longer lasting—the deepening creep of roots underneath. And when you catch a glimpse of these things, give thanks and keep going.

"AHEAD OF US IS A HOME OF SECURITY AND COMFORT THAT WILL NOT DISAPPOINT US, AND FOR WHICH THE ASKING PRICE HAS ALREADY BEEN PAID IN FULL."

#ISTHISIT

## 4. PRAY

*Be ... faithful in prayer. (v 12)*

How often do you pray for other people in your church? If you're anything like me, the answer is "Not enough". Few of us could describe ourselves as "faithful in prayer"—but all of us can make a start at being *more* faithful in prayer.

One thing I've found helpful is the free app for phones and tablets called Prayer Mate. I have set it up to cycle through the names of the people in my Bible-study group, giving me a different person to pray for every day, which helps to keep them in mind while they're out of sight for most of the week. Make a habit of praying for the preacher on a Saturday night or Sunday morning, or make it part of your drive to church. When you're doing small talk with someone after church on a Sunday, finish (or start) the conversation by asking, "How can I pray for you this week?"

It's as we pray for people that we become invested in their lives. The more consistently we pray for people, the more consistently we'll love them—and that's when church will feel like home.

## 5. SHARE

*Share with the Lord's people who are in need. Practise hospitality. (v 13)*

Most of us associate hospitality with lavish Sunday lunches at someone's house after church—which, depending on your housing situation, may not be feasible. I receive far more hospitality than I give. Sometimes that makes me feel guilty, but mostly it makes me feel grateful—one day I hope to be able to pay it forward.

Now, I love roast dinners. But that's not a full description of what hospitality *is*. At the heart of hospitality are the principles of *allowing ourselves to be known* (by letting others onto our home turf) and *spending ourselves for the sake of others* (by laying on food and drink at our own expense). Both of those things can be done in a way that doesn't involve inviting people to eat Sunday lunch sitting on your bed in your studio flat (though, why not?!). It just requires a little creative thinking. Is there one person you could have over for an easy week-night tea or a take-away? If your place is small, take a picnic to a park. Or see if you can team up with other people at church—maybe a single person or a busy family—to help them host at their house. Don't make the mistake of thinking that welcoming others must wait till you have the semi-detached place with easy parking for guests.

## KEEP LONGING

Our longing for home is a good thing, even if sometimes it's a hard thing. That sense of rootlessness gives us an opportunity to live radically, like Jesus; and to remember where home really is. In many ways, it's actually easier for a sofa-surfing Christian to embrace that truth than it is for a mortgaged-to-the-hilt homeowner.

Because for every subject of the kingdom of Christ, home is not here, but it is ahead of us—a home of security and comfort that will not disappoint us, and for which the asking price has already been paid in full.

And wonderfully, we get a taste of it on the journey, Sunday by Sunday, as we drive home for Christmas together.

# 4. NOSTALGIA & REGRET

## REMEMBER THAT TIME WHEN...? / I WISH I COULD FORGET

"That was fun," I said. "I'm glad we decided to come in the end."

"Yeah, me too."

My friend Ruby and I had been to a get-together for a friend of ours from university who was getting married—and now we were setting off on the four-hour drive home.

It had been a good day. We'd reminisced about the student Bible study where we'd all met; the people who'd shaped us; the adventures we'd been on. We'd remembered the times spent poring over the Bible in a cosy living room; the afternoons spent cooking in the church kitchen; the Sunday evenings spent watching TV in somebody's house with a cup of tea (I know—it was wild).

"Ahh, Manchester," I said, looking wistfully out of the window as the once-familiar city landscape of red-bricked terraced houses thinned out into suburbs.

"Look at it. I feel... I feel..."

I searched for a profound word that would capture my emotions.

"I feel... erm... sad?"

Ruby smiled. "What you feel, Rachel, is nostalgic."

She was right. Nostalgia was precisely what I was feeling.

The word "nostalgia" comes from two Greek words which nicely capture the pull of this emotion: *nostos*, meaning "to return home", and *algos*, meaning "pain"—the same word that gives us the medical term "myalgia" for muscle pain. And if we're suffering from nostalgia myalgia, it's our hearts that are aching.

## A WARM SADNESS

It's a strange emotion, nostalgia. On the one hand, there's a warmth and fondness as we remember good times and happy seasons. But at the same time, there's a sadness that comes from knowing that those moments now exist only in our memory, and we'll never get them back again. Nostalgia is a longing "to return home"—whatever familiar, happy, safe time and place "home" is for us—mixed with the pain of knowing that we can't. It's a recognition of the slow march of time that we are powerless to stop.

The pull of nostalgia lies behind much of our popular culture. It's the reason you click on those Buzzfeed articles about "13 Breakfast Cereals that Every 90s Kid Will Remember" or "17 Stationery Items We Need to Bring Back". And nostalgia explains why my friendship group from when I was at school—now grown-up women with grown-up jobs and relationships—have a continuing obsession with all things Harry Potter. It's the franchise that never dies.

Nostalgia is evident in our fashion and music choices too. Sales of vinyl records recently reached a 25-year high. However we listen to them, we love the old songs that take us back to our youth, and the new ones that play off that feeling. We can't help but smile as we sing along to Ed Sheeran's chorus in "Castle On The Hill".

Every generation gets nostalgic eventually, but I wonder whether technology has prompted ours to embrace the feeling sooner than any before us. Social media likes to remind us of what we were doing on this day three, five or ten years ago— as we look down at our phones on the way to our adult jobs, we smile wistfully as we see a younger, more carefree version of ourselves grinning back at us. We can share pop-culture memes from our childhood at the press of a button. Streaming means that we're able to re-watch the old sitcoms we used to turn on when we got home from school. It's ironic that it's the new tech in our hands which stirs our longing for a simpler, bygone, tech-free era.

Now, there are some ways in which this culture of collective nostalgia is harmless fun. But has it ever struck you as a bit, well... odd? If I and thousands of others are spending our spare time reading about pencil sharpeners from 20 years ago, clearly something is going on deep in our psyche. And it's not always helpful (the something going on, that is, not the pencil sharpeners—they remain useful, even in an iphone era). Sometimes our obsession with the past masks an uneasy relationship with our present and a fear about our future. As the writer of Ecclesiastes puts it:

> *Do not say, "Why were the old days better than these?"*
> *For it is not wise to ask such questions.*
>
> *(Ecclesiastes 7 v 10)*

But nostalgia isn't the only way we look back on our lives so far, because nostalgia looks back on happy times. And, of course, all of us have moments in our past that weren't so rosy—things we did, or that were done to us, which we regret or lament.

For some of us, these regrets continue to cloud our existence years later. We wonder how the direction of our life would have changed if we'd made a different decision—would we be in a better place now?

Perhaps there were relationships that went too far or broke off too soon; or jobs or opportunities you missed out on or turned down. *If only I'd known... If only I'd said... If only I'd done things differently.* Perhaps you've carried a secret into your 20s—a mistake you made or a wound that was inflicted on you by someone else—and it still chews you up inside. You're left wondering if you'll ever be able to move on from it. (And it's worth saying right here that if that wound was caused by some kind of abuse or neglect, you need much more than this chapter. Please speak to a trusted Christian friend or pastor instead.)

As we consider our past, often we're stuck between these two slightly (or severely) unpleasant emotions.

Nostalgia says, *I wish I could relive that time in my life.*

Regret says, *I wish I could undo that time in my life.*

But the truth is, we can't do either. Neither mindset is going to help us flourish as adults. Surely there's a better way of looking back on the past? After all, it can never be too soon to find out—the longer we live, the more we will have to look back on. It's well worth making peace with our past.

## PINING FOR THOSE GOLDEN TEMPLE DAYS

There's a curious incident tucked away in the Old Testament book of Ezra. At this point in Bible history, the Israelites had been defeated by the superpower of the day, Babylon. Their country had been brought to ruin, and their best people were carried away to live in exile in a foreign country. In Babylon, God's people spent 70 long years pining for Israel, the land of their forefathers, until finally, in the book of Ezra, they got to go home.

The first thing the returned exiles did when they got back to Jerusalem was to set about rebuilding the ransacked temple—the building that was at the centre of Jewish worship. The temple was the place where the living God had dwelled in glory, and where his people could commune with him. At this stage, the people were led by a man named Zerubbabel (Ezra himself didn't come into it until later). They rebuilt the altar, so that they could start sacrificing to God straight away. And then—in a great show of pageantry—they laid the foundations for the temple itself.

The whole description is meant to echo the golden age in Israel's history over 500 years previously when Solomon built the first temple (an era that was sort of the Israelite equivalent of the 90s. Or the 00s, if you're really young). Just like Solomon did, the returning exiles brought in the best tradesmen and shipped in the building supplies from Tyre and Lebanon. And just like Solomon did, they started work in the second month of the Jewish calendar—a time when the rains were starting to ease and the fields were full of food to be harvested.

When they gathered to celebrate the foundation being successfully laid, they even put on some throwback tunes. The priests and Levites put on their gladrags, struck up the trumpets and cymbals, and sang the same song that was sung to celebrate the dedication of Solomon's temple:

*"[God] is good; his love towards Israel endures for ever."*

*And all the people gave a great shout of praise to the* LORD, *because the foundation of the house of the* LORD *was laid.*

*(Ezra 3 v 11)*

It was a great homecoming moment for God's people—and yet the celebration was tinged with sadness:

*But many of the older priests and Levites and family heads, who had seen the former temple, wept aloud when they saw the foundation of this temple being laid, while many others shouted for joy. No one could distinguish the sound of the shouts of joy from the sound of weeping, because the people made so much noise. And the sound was heard far away.*

*(v 12-13)*

These older Israelites remembered the glorious temple of Solomon's day—and they cried, because this new one paled in comparison. It was much smaller, much less lavish. It wasn't only this building, either—Israel's whole status on the world stage had been dramatically reduced, and their slightly limp temple was just one sign of that. The old guard knew that things were better in the days before the exile. So instead of total celebration, we get this scene of mingled joy and sadness—kind of like my nostalgic car ride home from Manchester.

For these older Israelites, it's likely these were tears not just of disappointment but of regret, too. After all, the reason the Israelites had been taken into exile was as punishment for their persistent disobedience. After King Solomon built his temple, things slowly unravelled because the Israelites began worshipping other, false gods. This new generation of Israelites would end up weeping again a few years later as they listened to the law being read, because they could see how woefully they and their ancestors had fallen short (Nehemiah 8 – 9). If only they'd listened to the warnings of the prophets. If only they'd changed their ways and turned back to the true God, the exile need never have happened and Solomon's temple would still be standing.

So as the old guard of Israelites stood in front of Zerubbabel's half-built temple and remembered days gone by, they wished they could relive them, and they wished they could undo them.

Of course, just like us, they couldn't do either.

But God didn't leave them there, stuck in a muddle of nostalgia and regret: he gave them words of comfort, hope and renewed purpose. He sent two prophets to speak to Zerubbabel and the rest of the Israelites about this whole disappointing-temple issue: Haggai and Zechariah. And both of them can help us to have a better attitude to the past, too.

## SMALL CAN BE BEAUTIFUL

The problem with pining for the past is that we risk missing what God's doing in the present. That's essentially what God says to the Israelites through Zechariah:

*Then the word of the LORD came to me: "The hands of Zerubbabel have laid the foundation of this temple; his hands will also complete it. Then you will know that the LORD Almighty has sent me to you.*

*"Who dares despise the day of small things, since the seven eyes of the LORD that range throughout the earth will rejoice when they see the chosen capstone in the hand of Zerubbabel?" (Zechariah 4 v 8-10)*

God described the Israelites' present as "the day of small things". He wasn't trying to sugarcoat the truth or convince them that now was better really. He didn't say, *You're remembering it all wrong. This temple is actually just as good as Solomon's. Sure it's different... but it's a good different.* No, this really was a day of small things and small temples.

And perhaps you feel like you're living in a day of small things too, and you wish you could go back to a time when things were bigger.

Maybe you're in a day that feels "small" spiritually—and you look back nostalgically on a period of your life when God seemed clearer or closer, and following Jesus seemed more exciting, and your efforts at church or evangelism were more effective.

Maybe you're in a day that feels "small" relationally—and you look back nostalgically to a season when you were in love for the first time, or your friendships seemed more fulfilling, or when you simply had the time and freedom to hang out a lot.

Maybe you're in a day that feels "small" physically—and you look back nostalgically to a time when you were healthier, or in less pain, or had the energy to do all the things you wanted.

And yes, maybe life now really is a day of small things. That's the way it goes sometimes. There's no point denying what was "big" in the past—there will certainly be some special times and golden moments that are behind you. But the solution is not to look back and grieve their passing, but to look back and give thanks that you had them at all.

While admitting what is "small" now, we need to be careful not to "despise" it—to do it down or wish it away or resent it. God is still at work in the day of small things. Zechariah gives us an extraordinary image of *God himself* rejoicing when his eyes see Zerubbabel placing the capstone in position to finish the temple. Here's the brilliant truth: we don't have to do "big things" to impress God. He's not so high and mighty that he's above our small things—instead, he works through them. And it makes God happy when we faithfully stick at his work, no matter how limp it looks in comparison to what's gone before. This is the stuff that makes God smile.

So yes, you might be in a day of small things—but don't despise it. If God's rejoicing, there's no room or reason for you to be resentful.

## GET ON BOARD

God doesn't just challenge how we *think* about the past and the present; through Haggai, he tells us that he transforms what we *do* in the present too.

> *The word of the LORD came through the prophet Haggai: "Speak to Zerubbabel son of Shealtiel, governor of Judah, to Joshua son of Jozadak, the high priest, and to the remnant of the people. Ask them, 'Who of you is left who saw this house in its former glory? How does it look to you now? Does it not seem to you like nothing? But now be strong, Zerubbabel,' declares the LORD. 'Be strong, Joshua son of Jozadak, the high priest. Be strong, all you people of the land,' declares the LORD, 'and work. For I am with you,' declares the LORD Almighty. 'This is what I covenanted with you when you came out of Egypt. And my Spirit remains among you. Do not fear.'" (Haggai 2 v 1-5)*

The danger was that Zerubbabel and the Israelites would get so discouraged by the sorry state of the temple compared to its heyday that they'd stop building and give up. So God gave them two clear commands: "Be strong ... and work". *Keep going.*

"THE BEST IS NOT BEHIND YOU. THE BEST IS YET TO COME."

#ISTHISIT

Why? Because God was with them. He reminded them that he had a "covenant" with them—a committed relationship of love which he would always stand by and stick to. He reminded them of what he'd done for them in the past in rescuing them from Egypt. And he reassured them that he was still with them by his Spirit—he was on their side.

When we're feeling awash with nostalgia, or cut up with regret, this is what we need reminding of too.

Sometimes it's helpful to look back. It's good to remember God's covenant with us, and the mighty things he's done in our past. We can reflect and rejoice over the way that he brought us to faith... the people he's used to grow us... the surprising way he's weaved together events... the changes he's made to our character... the things he's used us to do. Don't take a trip down memory lane without stopping to admire these flowers of God's grace along the way. They will certainly be there, even if there are painful nettles in the undergrowth too.

Yet our remembering is not primarily meant to leave us with a warm fuzzy glow; it's meant to help us to "be strong ... and work".

Sometimes, we so want to recapture our past that we make stupid decisions in an attempt to claw it back. *Maybe I should move back to Manchester?* I think to myself wistfully. *Or, like, take a gap year before I get too old?* But neither of those things are a very good idea right now.

Perhaps you're tempted to quit a stressful job or back out of a difficult relationship. And while both of those might be wise things to do, they're not a good strategy for winding back the clock. I mentioned in Chapter Two that God has put us where he wants us, and there are specific "good works" which he has "prepared in advance for us to do" (Ephesians 2 v 10). Some of them will be hard—but all of them are worth doing, and in all of them we are empowered by God's Spirit.

So stop living in the past, and look for the people you can love and the good works you can do in the present. Be strong and work.

## WHAT LIES AHEAD

God goes on to say something else through Haggai too. Essentially, *This isn't it. The best is yet to come.*

Remember, the celebration of the new temple echoed the dedication of Solomon's temple. But there was one significant thing missing. If we rewind to 2 Chronicles, we see that in Solomon's day there was a very different response to that song of praise:

> *The singers raised their voices in praise to the LORD and sang:*
> *"He is good;*
> *his love endures for ever."*
> *Then the temple of the LORD was filled with the cloud, and the priests could not perform their service because of the cloud, for the glory of the LORD filled the temple of God.*
> *(2 Chronicles 5 v 13-14)*

The high point of Solomon's celebration was this supernatural cloud descending on the temple. It was a symbol of God's real, awesome, majestic, mysterious presence. God was with them, in a very real and unmistakable way.

So part of what was so disappointing about Zerubbabel's temple was that no such glory cloud descended—not when the foundations were laid, and not when it was finished, either.

Without God's glory filling it, the building wasn't glorious at all—it was mostly disappointing.

That's why what God said through Haggai next is so significant:

*This is what the LORD Almighty says: "In a little while I will once more shake the heavens and the earth, the sea and the dry land. I will shake all nations, and what is desired by all nations will come, and I will fill this house with glory," says the LORD Almighty. "The silver is mine and the gold is mine," declares the LORD Almighty.*

*"The glory of this present house will be greater than the glory of the former house," says the LORD Almighty. "And in this place I will grant peace," declares the LORD Almighty.*
(Haggai 2 v 6-9)

God basically said, *Yes, things now are unimpressive. But the best is not behind you. The best is yet to come. This isn't it yet.* The Israelites didn't need to pine for the good old days of Solomon's temple, because something was coming that would be even "greater than the glory of the former house" (v 9).

Fast-forward 600 years and Jesus' disciples are overwhelmed—not underwhelmed—by the appearance of the temple (Mark 13 v 1—it had had another makeover since Zerubbabel's day, yet God's glory still hadn't come to dwell in it). But Jesus was never particularly impressed by it. He looked at it and said, "Destroy this temple, and I will raise it again in three days" (John 2 v 19). In other words, *This isn't it yet. Something better is coming.*

Later, the disciples realised what that something better was— "the temple [Jesus] had spoken of was his body" (v 21). The Old Testament temple was about providing a way for sinful people to come into the presence of God in peace. That's why the Israelites had been performing daily animal sacrifices there for hundreds of years. But it was all pointing to the moment when Jesus' body—broken on the cross and raised to life three days later—achieved peace with God once and for all. That's why, when Jesus appeared to his friends after his resurrection, the first thing he said was, "Peace be with you!" (20 v 19). It's through his sacrifice of himself that anyone, from anywhere in the world, can come into God's presence in peace in prayer, and can go into God's presence in peace beyond death.

No wonder God told Zerubbabel, *The best is yet to come.*

And there's a sense in which he says that to us today, too. However much it might feel to the contrary, the best is not behind you. No—the best is yet to come.

In the book of Revelation at the end of the Bible, we're given a picture of what it will be like for us to come into God's personal presence in peace in heaven. Just as the prophet Haggai spoke about the arrival of something "desired by all nations", in Revelation the apostle John sees "a great multitude that no one could count, from every nation, tribe, people and language, standing before the throne and before the Lamb" (Revelation 7 v 9). This multitude are the people "who have come out of the great tribulation; they have washed their robes and made them white in the blood of the Lamb" (v 14)—Christians, those who have stayed faithful to Christ in all the muddle and mess and misery of life in this world. And this is what life is like for them now, in heaven:

> They are before the throne of God
>   and serve him day and night in his temple;
> and he who sits on the throne
>   will shelter them with his presence.
> "Never again will they hunger;
>   never again will they thirst.

*The sun will not beat down on them,"*
  *nor any scorching heat.*
*For the Lamb at the centre of the throne*
  *will be their shepherd;*
*"he will lead them to springs of living water."*
  *"And God will wipe away every tear from their eyes."*
                                        *(7 v 15-17)*

I don't know what it is that's not working in your life right now—the things which make you want to go back to a happier, easier era. I don't know what you wish you could go back in time to change. But I do know that whatever's behind you, if you're a Christian—if you've been washed clean "in the blood of the Lamb"—then this is the future that awaits you on the other side of the grave.

It's a future where you will enjoy being sheltered by God's presence, completely safe and free from fear. A future without any material or physical need. A future that is free from any relational or spiritual sense of longing, because Christ shepherds you to living water that satisfies. A future where the painful memories and fraught "if onlys" all fade as God himself wipes away your tears of regret.

This is a time worth longing for. And it lies ahead of you, not behind.

Are you suffering from an unhealthy nostalgia myalgia? One way to tell is if you're longing more for your past than you are for this future. If you spend more time reading articles about 90s stationery than you do dwelling on what God has prepared for you in eternity, it's time to shift your gaze.

The past may have been rosy or it may have been miserable, and it was probably a mix of both. You may well be in a "day of small things" right now. And, yes, it's possible that your best time on this earth lies in your past.

But keep your eyes fixed forward, not on what's behind. Because one thing is certain: your best days are yet to come.

# 5. I HATE MY JOB
## I'VE GOT *HOW* LONG TILL I CAN RETIRE?!

Question: What will you spend 92,120 hours of your life doing?

Answer: Working.

And it sure often feels that way, right?

So, as we consider the reality of 92k hours spent working, some of us get out the clock, and some of us reach for the ladder.

The clock marks the time until we can stop working and do something fun instead.

We count down the hours until the end of the day, the days until the end of the week, the weeks until our big trip-of-the-year, and the years until we can retire. A friend told me about someone he met at a barbecue recently who had a countdown on his phone: 368 months until retirement. (To which I thought, *Is that all? His pension fund must be in a better state than mine…*) While it's sad to imagine someone wishing away the next 30 years of their existence, I'm sure I fall into this mindset more often than I realise. Most of us, I suspect, are natural clock-watchers at heart.

But that's a depressing way to live. If we're going to spend so many of our waking hours working, we might as well get something out of it. So we reach for the ladder, constantly looking for the way to climb a little bit higher in our chosen career. We plan ahead to the next project, or the next promotion, or the next company, searching for an opportunity to leap to the next rung. And people in their 20s and early 30s tend to leap pretty often; these days it's typical for graduates to have done four different jobs by the time they're 32.

But sometimes the ladder turns out not to be a ladder at all—it's more like the moving staircases at Hogwarts School of Witchcraft and Wizardry, of Harry Potter fame. Everyone else seems to know how to navigate them—but you feel like one of those confused first-year students because none of your efforts at moving up get you to where you want to go. You were aiming for a career in journalism, but instead you've ended up in an obscure part of the castle doing data entry for a manager like Moaning Myrtle. You're stuck on the bottom rung of the wrong ladder. Or maybe you're struggling to get any work at all.

If there's one thing that marks our generation out from our forebears, it's a desire not only to have work but for our work to mean something. We want work to pay the bills (and these days, it's not a given that it will), but we also want work to fulfil us. An ad I saw on the side of a bus for a job website played off the Madness song from the 90s with the slogan, "Mondays. It must be love." The implication is clear: you must love what you do—and if you don't, you owe it to yourself to find work that you do love.

Yet so often, we find ourselves disappointed. The polling company Gallup found that only 29% of us are "engaged" at work—in other words, less than a third of us are emotionally invested in our jobs. Why does something we want to love turn out to be so hard to love?

## IT'S MEANT TO FEEL GOOD

It's right to want work to be fulfilling—because it is meant to be fulfilling. As with many areas of life, we can trace the root of our conflicted career aspirations back to the first pages of human history.

You're probably familiar with Genesis 1, where God makes stuff and it's good. But Genesis 2 gives us a slowed-down account of the creation process. Verse 5 picks up the story partway through:

> *Now no shrub had yet appeared on the earth and no plant had yet sprung up, for the LORD God had not sent rain on the earth and there was no one to work the ground...*

God is planning to turn his blank canvas of creation into a beautiful, abundant garden. But he's missing two things: water and a worker. So...

> *... streams came up from the earth and watered the whole surface of the ground. Then the LORD God formed a man from the dust of the ground and breathed into his nostrils the breath of life, and the man became a living being.*
>
> *Now the LORD God had planted a garden in the east, in Eden; and there he put the man he had formed ... The LORD God took the man and put him in the Garden of Eden to work it and take care of it. (v 6-8, 15)*

So now there's water and a worker. But something is *still* missing: a woman. It turns out that one worker is not enough:

> *The LORD God said, "It is not good for the man to be alone. I will make a helper suitable for him." (v 18)*

And after a bit of invasive surgery for Adam, the woman is formed. So now there are two autonomous human beings, with different strengths and skills but the same mission. Because, as they might tell you on a team-building company awayday, teamwork makes the dream work. And God has set out his big dream for humanity in 1 v 27-28:

> *... God created mankind in his own image,*
>   *in the image of God he created them;*
>   *male and female he created them.*
>
> *God blessed them and said to them, "Be fruitful and increase in number; fill the earth and subdue it. Rule over the fish in the sea and the birds in the sky and over every living creature that moves on the ground." (v 27-28)*

Work is part of what God has tasked us to do, as human beings made in his image. Just as God spent six days filling and ordering creation, in these verses he turns creation over to human beings to carry on filling it and ordering it. The man and woman are to make babies and make decisions; to grow food and grow ideas; to organise animals and organise celebrations.

This is why work is *meant* to feel good and sometimes *does* feel good. This is why it's a thrill when we hit a target—we're working in the image of God. This is why it feels good when we work with others to achieve something together that we couldn't on our own—we're working in the image of God. This is why it's satisfying when we finish a project—we're working in the image of God. This is why it puts a spring in our step when our work makes someone else's life better—we're working in the image of God.

"I DON'T KNOW HOW MUCH YOUR BOSS VALUES YOU. BUT I KNOW HOW MUCH YOUR LORD DOES."

#ISTHISIT

And this means that whatever work we do—even if we're underemployed, underpaid or under-appreciated—if we're doing the job of filling and ordering creation then that work is worthwhile, because we're working in the image of God.

Work is, and can be, and should be wonderful.

And yet... so often, it's not. And Genesis tells us why that is, too.

## FROM GARDENING TO BATTLING

The man and woman decided they wanted something other than the job God had given them. They wanted to be "like God"—sitting in his office and calling the shots themselves (3 v 5). So they ate the fruit they'd been commanded not to, and with their disobedience, creation came crashing down around them. Work has never been perfectly satisfying since.

In Genesis 3 God spelled out the consequences of their sin:

> *Cursed is the ground because of you;*
> *through painful toil you will eat food from it*
> *all the days of your life.*
> *It will produce thorns and thistles for you,*
> *and you will eat the plants of the field.*
> *By the sweat of your brow*
> *you will eat your food*
> *until you return to the ground,*
> *since from it you were taken;*
> *for dust you are*
> *and to dust you will return. (Genesis 3 v 17-19)*

Sin's entry into the world brought curse into God's blessing. Humanity's God-given gardening project became a battle with the elements. What was once an exciting task marked by joy and abundance became a fight to survive marked by pain and frustration. The man and woman's perfect working relationship was wrecked by conflict, blame-shifting and power struggles.

The sin in us, and the sin around us, is the reason why work is so often so horrible. Our colleagues gossip or our boss is overbearing—it's work under the curse. We feel overwhelmed as we look at a to-do list we'll never get to the end of—it's work under the curse. We make mistakes through negligence or through honest error—it's work under the curse. Our hard work only serves to make rich people richer—it's work under the curse. Our labour is just plain boring—it's work under the curse. And the list goes on...

Genesis 1 – 3 shows us that our careers are lived out under the two realities of God's image and God's curse. We experience both.

Knowing this leaves us with realistic expectations for work. Sometimes work will feel good—and in the moments that it does, rejoice. As you come home from a good day at work, thank God that he has made you in his image to work in his world. Good work is an exceptional gift. Since your sin is part of what's wrong with the world, satisfying work is never the least you deserve—no, it's always more than you deserve. Don't take it for granted.

But a lot of the time, work will not feel good. This is not because something has gone particularly wrong—this is normal in a post-Genesis-3 world.

## WHAT TO DO IF YOU HATE YOUR JOB

OK, so work sometimes sucks—but how do you deal with that? What are you meant to do if you really do hate your job?

The Bible doesn't speak directly to our careers, but there are places where it speaks to those who endured a far lower status than low-paid, entry-level workers today: slaves. Here's what Paul says to Christian slaves in the Greek city of Corinth:

> *Were you a slave when you were called [to follow Christ]?*
> *Don't let it trouble you—although if you can gain your*
> *freedom, do so. For the one who was a slave when called to*
> *faith in the Lord is the Lord's freed person; similarly, the one*
> *who was free when called is Christ's slave. You were bought*
> *at a price; do not become slaves of human beings. Brothers*
> *and sisters, each person, as responsible to God, should*
> *remain in the situation they were in when God called them.*
> (1 Corinthians 7 v 21-24)

(Side note: Yes, slavery in the Bible feels like an awkward and uncomfortable topic. Yes, there are good answers out there. No, we don't have space for them here—suggested resources are on page 205).

Paul says that, contrary to popular belief, Christians are by and large free to do what they want—including when it comes to our careers. If it's not sinful, you're free to do it.

If you hate your job, you are free to look for a new one. You're free to try something completely new. Some of us are prone to playing the martyr, staying in miserable situations because we feel that must be where God wants us, and we feel guilty about doing something to change it. But Paul says, "If you can gain your freedom, do so" (v 21)—*if you want a new job and you can find one, go for it.*

That's what my friend Will learned:

> "I remember a couple of years ago speaking to my pastor
> when I had reached the end of my tolerance for existential

*despair. I had decided enough was enough; I was sick of my job, but felt trapped because I thought that in order to justify leaving I had to go on to something bigger and better. Whatever was next needed to be something that everyone would respond to with, 'Well done Will—it's about time you got a proper job'. But my pastor told me to apply for the first equivalent job I saw, and just get a change of scenery and head space. So I did. God graciously provided me with a new job and with it, a total change of pace, colleagues and atmosphere. I was so much happier. Sometimes you've got to try something new, and don't worry if it's not massively grandiose."*

"If you can gain your freedom, do so"—but at the same time, in the very same verse, "Don't let it trouble you". However stressful it is, or boring it is, or difficult it is—don't let your job get you down. Our pursuit of "freedom" from a particular job should never become all-consuming. While we're often *free* to move job, it's not always *good* to move job—because, in the long run, Paul says that it really doesn't matter that much. And there are other things that matter much more: not least, having the time and energy to be a good friend, to honour your family and to serve your church.

I don't know how much your boss values you. But I do know how much your Lord does. He's "bought" you "at a price" (v 23). And the price was his own life. And it's *this* truth that has the power to transform our mindset on work. Christ has paid what we couldn't—a life lived in perfect obedience to his Father—to set us free. Regardless of how oppressed or worn down we might feel, this is the Christian's status: "the Lord's freed person" (v 22). Imagine how liberating it must have felt to hear that as a slave in Paul's time.

And ultimately, this is what matters. If you're a Christian, your employment status does not define you. The approval or disappointment of people about your working life—be it that of your boss or your parents or you yourself—doesn't ultimately matter. Whether your job title is "slave" or "master"—or "intern" or "sales assistant" or "doctor" or "PR Co-ordinator" or "call-centre worker" or "structural engineer"—in God's eyes you are the Lord's freed person.

This is what gives us hope, even joy, on Monday mornings. However much you feel like you're floundering, and however toxic the environment in your workplace is, you can walk in there with your head held high—and, having worked hard and with integrity, you can leave again eight/ten/twelve hours later with your head still held high. You are the Lord's free person.

## SIX TIPS FOR A HAPPIER WORKING LIFE

But we're not just the Lord's freed person—we're also "Christ's slave[s]" (v 22). We should expect to graft for him. When you became a Christian, it's not like you and God became partners in a law firm; he was, and remains, the one in charge. He bought you with a price, so he has a right to tell you how to live your life—and how to work your job. And when it comes to our careers, it's not so much what we do that God's interested in, as the way that we do it.

In his letter to the church in Colossae, Paul gives some instructions to a different group of Christian slaves. His advice is as sound today as it was two thousand ago. Living God's way doesn't only honour him—it's also always the happiest and healthiest thing for us in the long run. So here are six tips for thriving in the workplace.

## 1. DO WHAT YOU'RE TOLD

*Slaves, obey your earthly masters in everything.*

*(Colossians 3 v 22)*

Something grates inside me when I read a verse like that. But Genesis 1 – 2 shows that order is built into God's creation. "The authorities that exist have been established by God" (Romans 13 v 1). Authority structures, whether in a nation, a church or a company, are a good thing in principle—even if in practice they are sometimes twisted to do great harm.

This means that your boss is your boss because God has made them your boss, and God wants you to do what they tell you. And at the start of our careers, there will inevitably be a lot of being told what to do. We've got to expect to work from the bottom up and earn trust and responsibility over time.

So "obey your earthly masters in everything"—even the instructions you don't like, or the instructions you think are just plain stupid. Don't look for ways to wriggle out of it. Don't turn every decision into a power struggle. Unless and until obedience to your earthly master comes at the cost of obedience to your heavenly one, just do what you're told.

## 2. BE SINCERE

*Obey your earthly masters ... not only when [their] eye is on you and to curry their favour, but with sincerity of heart.*

*(Colossians 3 v 22)*

To be "sincere" is to be the same person on the inside as on the outside: so the hard-working, respectful, professional exterior we put on is meant to be matched by a hard-working, respectful interior attitude. If that is true of us, we will work in the same way when our boss is in the room as we do when they are out of it.

So when you're tempted to gossip or moan about someone at work, don't. When you find yourself rehearsing a long internal monologue of what you would like to say to your boss, stop. When you're tempted to slack off while your manager is in a meeting, resist. Be sincere.

And if, like me, your heart is not sincere most of the time—if you care more about what people think of you than you care about people themselves—remember that one of the best ways to grow in genuine love for people is to pray for them. Every day as you get ready for work, pray for your colleagues and your boss, and ask God to give you a sincerity of heart towards others.

## 3. FEAR GOD, NOT PEOPLE
*... and with reverence for the Lord. (v 22)*

Perhaps you admire your colleagues and desperately want them to think well of you. Or perhaps you work with an absolute dragon and just desperately want to avoid getting shouted at. Either way, I suspect that much of our motivation in the workplace comes down to fear. How does fear manifest itself for you?

Paul says that we're to work "with reverence for the Lord"—an awe and respect that comes from knowing that he's the one in control of the universe, and that ultimately it's his opinion which matters. If we fear God, not people, we won't work crazy long hours in an attempt to prove ourselves; we won't tell white lies to cover our tracks; and we won't cave when we're under pressure to do something sinful—even if refusing will harm our career prospects.

And if we're fearing God, not people, this also means that we'll be bold in sharing the gospel at work. We'll seek to speak about

Jesus, because we'll care more about what our co-workers think of him than what they think of us, and we'll care more about what's best for them than what's comfortable for us. And if people are disinterested or hostile, that won't matter—because we're not afraid of them. We fear God.

## 4. TRY HARD

*Whatever you do, work at it with all your heart, as working for the Lord, not human masters. (v 23)*

If Jesus rocked up to your workplace tomorrow, how would you act? Imagine he donned the manager's uniform or chaired the team meeting. How would that affect your attitude?

Well, he's already there. The reality is that you're not only working for human masters—you're working for the Lord. He gave his very best for you—his own life and perfect righteousness—and now you're called to give your very best to him. And the place where we "work for the Lord" isn't just at church on a Sunday but in our jobs on a Monday. So "whatever you do", do your best at it—whether it's stacking shelves or trading stocks (and if you think that one of those is more important than the other, then you've got your view of work wrong).

Chances are that your job is a mixture of the interesting and the tedious. All of it is to be done with all of your heart. Don't do the bare minimum. Don't cut corners. Actively look for ways to do your job better or to make your organisation operate more effectively. Do everything you can to make your working environment a better place for others to be.

## 5. WORK FOR A BONUS THAT LASTS

*You know that you will receive an inheritance from the Lord as a reward. It is the Lord Christ you are serving. (v 24)*

I increasingly have the feeling that all my friends have more money than me. And as I look at their lifestyles and imagine their salaries (and hear about their important-sounding job titles and staff perks and parties), I sit at my own desk feeling resentful.

When that happens, I need a reality check. I earn more than 97% of other people on the planet—am I really going to complain? And more than that, I need to remember that God has something better in store. I'm heading for a heavenly "inheritance that can never perish, spoil or fade"—an eternity of physical and spiritual satisfaction (1 Peter 1 v 4). This treasure in heaven will outshine and outlast even the most outrageous bonus. Being God's chosen heir beats being employee of the month.

If you give your life to faithfully serving Christ, this is what you're promised too. When we take the long view, money now doesn't matter all that much; nor does the kudos that comes with climbing the ladder. The greatest potential rewards of your career lie beyond its end—not in retirement, but in eternity.

## 6. REMEMBER JUSTICE IS COMING
*Anyone who does wrong will be repaid for their wrongs, and there is no favouritism. (Colossians 3 v 25)*

People at work are going to screw you over. If they haven't already, they will one day. They're going to take the credit for your good idea; they're going to pin the blame on you when it wasn't your fault; they're going to make jokes at your expense; they're going to discredit your reputation; they're going to pass over you for opportunities; they're going to go back on their word.

Life is not fair. And while there is a place for taking grievances through official channels—especially where people have acted against us or against others in a way that is harmful and/or il-legal—we'll sometimes find that justice is not done in the way that we want it to be.

When that happens (and we can assume it happened pretty regularly for slaves in first-century Turkey), we can take comfort in the fact that a day of perfect justice is coming. Your grievance may have been overlooked or brushed aside, but God saw it, and he cares about it. He promises that those who have wronged you will be repaid for their wrongs. There will be no hint of favouritism or cronyism on that day. Total justice will be done.

Don't carry around grudges and bitterness. These will only eat you up inside and make you more miserable. Instead, entrust the hurts you've experienced to God, talk to him about how it's not fair, and give thanks that one day he will deal with it.

## MONDAYS. IT CAN BE LOVE.

It's really hard to work like this, especially in a workplace culture where nobody else does. It's hard to get up day after day to go to a job you don't really like. But it's better—far better—than looking at the clock or reaching for the ladder.

When the alarm rings in the morning, it's waking you up to a new day as the Lord's freed person—a new day where you have the privilege of serving Christ in your work. And one new day soon, God will reverse the curse of Genesis 3 and you'll spend an eternity working productively, in total perfection, reflecting the image of God.

Seek ultimate fulfilment in your work, and you'll always end up frustrated—the ladder will never reach high enough. Seek ultimate fulfilment in the weekend, and work will only get in the way—the clock will never move fast enough. But seek fulfilment in the God who created work as good, and you'll be free to enjoy what work offers with gratitude, and ride out the frustrations that work brings with joy.

"Mondays. It must be love." And it can be love—when you go to work for the One you love, because he has loved you.

# 6. DOUBT

## IS GOD EVEN REAL OR
## AM I WASTING MY LIFE?

Sometimes I close my eyes to pray and I get this horrible feeling that there's nobody there.

The sensation is extremely unpleasant—there's a physical churning in my stomach and an accompanying anxious tightness in my chest. It's as if I'm on a cliff edge, staring into the emptiness below.

I tend to go through phases where I feel like this for a few days or a week or so, and then it fades. It's deeply unnerving.

The feeling is probably most unpleasant when I'm at church. On the outside, I look like everyone else, singing along. As I look around, it's easy to believe I'm the only soul in the room who ever feels this way inside.

I've talked to a lot of people about a lot of topics in this book (some of them under duress). People have talked about a lack of direction, or career anxiety, or the sense of loss that comes with being single for longer than you anticipated. But only a few people have talked about doubt.

That's because doubt is something that's hard to admit to, hard to talk about, and hard to buy a book about. But it does happen—I'm not the only one, and neither are you.

I suspect it's pretty common to wonder, after a few years of being a Christian as an adult, whether you've got it right at all—to find yourself with nagging questions, uncertainties and grey areas that won't go away. Maybe one of these rings true for you:

- You watched a documentary or read some articles that raised intellectual questions for you. Maybe the Bible isn't accurate—does it contradict itself? Are the miracles just ancient folklore? How can we square the creation account with science?

- For the first time in your life, you're actually suffering—tragedy or illness has hit you or someone you love. How could God let that happen? You're starting to wonder whether he really cares, or just isn't there.

- You look at other Christians who are on fire for God—they just seem to really, really love Jesus. You look at yourself and think, "I'm not like that. What's wrong with me? Maybe I'm not a Christian after all." (This is better described as a lack of assurance.)

- You fell in love with the wrong person, made some choices that you knew the God you grew up with wouldn't like, and stopped going to church because it made you feel guilty. Now you don't know how to come back or even if you want to—you're wondering if God's there at all.

- The more you read the Bible, the more you discover things you don't like. Maybe someone you love who wasn't a Christian has died—it's easier to believe that God isn't real than to believe that there's a God who sends people to hell.

- You're struggling with a sin you just can't stop. You know the theory about being indwelled by the Holy Spirit. But how can that be true when you can't stop watching porn or arguing with your spouse? Surely if this were all real, you'd be able to change?

- You grew up in a Christian home, and as you look back, you realise there wasn't ever a decisive moment when you started following Jesus—it's more that you just didn't stop. You've never experienced any supernatural fizzes and bangs. So how can you tell that your faith is real? Are you only a Christian because everyone around you is—would it be different if you'd grown up somewhere like Saudi Arabia?

If you're in your 20s and experiencing doubt, then now is the time to deal with it. After all, if God's *not* real you had better decide that now, in your 20s, so that you can spend the rest of your life enjoying brunch on a Sunday morning instead of standing in church singing to a deity that doesn't exist. If you only live once, you should live once while having more money, more holidays and more sex.

But if this whole Christian thing *is* real (and, for the record, I'm convinced that it is), then doubt will rob us of all sense of joy in following Christ. It will hold us back from living in sold-out service of Jesus, and from the blessings that flow from that.

The good news is that God doesn't want us to doubt, and so his word speaks about doubt. In some places the Bible addresses doubters in quite forceful terms; there's a kind of doubt that is deceitful and dangerous because it's a sign of wanting to keep a foot in both camps (for example, James 1 v 6-8). But there are other places in the Bible which address honest, struggling doubters with great patience and kindness. Think of the way that Jesus speaks to "doubting Thomas" after his resurrection: "Put your finger here; see my hands. Reach out your hand and put it into my side. Stop doubting and believe" (John 20 v 27). Jesus is gentle and understanding of Thomas's weak faith, yet he still calls Thomas to move away from it.

In the Christian life some doubt is to be expected—but it is never to be embraced.

OK, but *how* do we follow Jesus' command to "stop doubting and believe"?

## CAN I SEE A(NOTHER) SIGN?

It's tempting to think that if we just had a little more proof—if God just made himself a little clearer—we'd be doubt-free. But countless incidents in the Gospels show that even when God walked on earth, people had a hard time believing in the One who stood in front of them.

One such episode is in John 6. At the start of the chapter, Jesus has fed a crowd of over 5,000 hungry people with just five loaves and two fish. This miracle-bread was as real to the senses and as satisfying to the stomach as anything you'll eat today. We know it must have been good, because the crowd come back for more the next day (and everything tastes better when it's free).

But this time round, Jesus serves up not another feast but some home truths:

*Jesus answered, "Very truly I tell you, you are looking for me, not because you saw the signs I performed but because you ate the loaves and had your fill. Do not work for food that spoils, but for food that endures to eternal life, which the Son of Man will give you. For on him God the Father has placed his seal of approval."*

*Then they asked him, "What must we do to do the works God requires?"*

*Jesus answered, "The work of God is this: to believe in the one he has sent."*

*So they asked him, "What sign then will you give that we may see it and believe you? What will you do?"*

*(John 6 v 26-30)*

This is astonishing. They had had a sign from Jesus less than 24 hours before—the whole loaves-and-fish thing. Now they're demanding another one, "that we may see it and believe"! Clearly, proof is not the problem. The problem is that they do not "believe in the one [God the Father] has sent"—Jesus.

Doubt is not an unimportant issue that can be swept under the rug, because at the heart of the Christian faith is not something you do ("What must we *do*?", v 28), but something you "believe" (v 29). Jesus is clear that we do have to have faith in him in order to have eternal life.

Of course, in order to doubt, you must have a faith to doubt in the first place. The experience of doubt does not mean that you are not a Christian. If your doubts make you feel uncomfortable, then that's probably because deep down you do want to believe. The problem comes when honest doubt becomes hardened disbelief. And it's the latter which Jesus comes up against next:

*Then Jesus declared, "I am the bread of life. Whoever comes to me will never go hungry, and whoever believes in me will never be thirsty. But as I told you, you have seen me and still you do not believe. All those the Father gives me will come to me, and whoever comes to me I will never drive away. For I have come down from heaven not to do my will but to do the will of him who sent me..."*

*At this the Jews there began to grumble about him because he said, "I am the bread that came down from heaven." They said, "Is this not Jesus, the son of Joseph, whose father and mother we know? How can he now say, 'I came down from heaven'?" (v 35-38, 41-42)*

People who aren't Christians—in this case, the Jews—will always think that Christianity sounds ridiculous. Don't let the scepticism of others unnerve you. Your colleagues will think that you're crazy. Your non-Christian friends and family will think that you're crazy. That's OK—Jesus has never and will never prove himself on the basis of popular opinion.

## HARD TEACHING

Yet as the conversation continues, it's Jesus' own disciples who start struggling to believe. As Jesus explains what he means by being "the bread of life", in a tricky few verses he says people must eat his flesh and drink his blood to have eternal life (v 43-59).

To us, this sounds slightly bizarre. But to Jesus' disciples, who were from a Jewish background and whose food rules banned consuming the blood of any animal, this was extremely offensive. That's why "on hearing it, many of his disciples said, 'This is a hard teaching. Who can accept it?'" (v 60).

Jesus' teaching has always been hard to accept. In our culture today, it's hard teaching that Jesus is the only way to God and that not all religions are equally valid. It's hard teaching that a God of justice sends people to hell. It's hard teaching that sex is reserved for one man and one woman within marriage.

When Jesus' teaching goes against the cultural current that we have been carried along by since the day we were born, we're tempted to think that it just cannot be true, let alone good. In the West today, the claims of Christ seem to be becoming more and more culturally abnormal—but in fact they've always been abnormal, from the moment he first spoke them.

Jesus' words have always been uncomfortable—but that doesn't make them untrue, and that doesn't make them not good. Far from it:

> *Aware that his disciples were grumbling about this, Jesus said to them, "Does this offend you? Then what if you see the Son of Man ascend to where he was before! The Spirit gives life; the flesh counts for nothing. The words I have spoken to you—they are full of the Spirit and life. Yet there are some of you who do not believe." For Jesus had known from the beginning which of them did not believe and who would betray him. (v 61-64)*

Jesus says that there's more to reality than what we can see—there's a spiritual dimension as well as a physical one. Again, this goes against the grain of our culture, which tends to tell us that if it's not measurable, it's not real. But Jesus is describing something which cannot be explained by scientific experiment, and doesn't need to be.

My brother Tim is a physics student. I once asked him if his studies ever challenged his faith, and he shrugged (in that way that little brothers never quite grow out of) and then said, "Not really. The thing that I keep coming back to is life. It's the great mystery of physics. What is it that makes me alive and conscious, and this coffee table not alive or conscious, when on an anatomical level we're made of the same things: protons, neutrons and electrons? There must be something more to it."

If physical life mystifies scientists, then it's hardly surprising that spiritual life—the "life" Jesus is talking about here—mystifies us even more. This life is given by the Spirit, who works through "the words [Jesus has] spoken to you" (v 62).

This is important to remember when we're wrestling with doubts—they won't be overcome by putting our fingers in our ears and backing away from everything Christian. If acknowledging our doubts makes us feel uncomfortable, it's tempting to occupy our minds with something else that doesn't. But this is the road to unbelief. If you want to be sure that God is real and that you are his child, you're going to need the Spirit to show you Christ, strengthen your faith and give you assurance. And Jesus' words are "full of the Spirit" (v 63)—so keep listening to them. Keep reading the Bible, and going to church to hear it taught, even when you feel like it's not doing anything for you. Ask God honestly: "I don't even know if you're there, but I'm praying to you so I guess part of me must believe you exist, and I'm asking: would you please speak to me by your word." Even when we don't feel much (or anything), if we believe Jesus, then we can know for sure that we have life.

And here's why...

## GOD'S GOT YOU

What qualifies you as a Christian is this: "If you declare with your mouth, 'Jesus is Lord,' and believe in your heart that

God raised him from the dead, you will be saved" (Romans 10 v 9). And if that's you—if you've asked Jesus to forgive your sins and you've committed to living with him as Lord of your life—then that is because "the Father has enabled" you:

*No one can come to me unless the Father has enabled them.*
*(John 6 v 65)*

But this truth makes some of us panic. We look at our lives—at our sin or our lack of excitement about being a Christian—and worry that perhaps we're not really Christians and never will be, because the Father hasn't called us. What if I'm just not "elect"? But this truth is meant to achieve the opposite—it's threaded throughout Scripture in order to give us assurance.

So how can you tell if you're a genuine Christian? Well, do you want to be one? Is there something in you (the Spirit) that makes you want to speak to God as your Father? That's a strong start. Think back over the years you've been following Jesus—has your life changed? Do you dislike sin, even if you still fall into it? Do you ask God for forgiveness? Do you wish that you loved others better?

If the answer to those questions is a hesitant "yes", then let this truth reassure you: God has called you, and he will not let you go. As Jesus said to that crowd:

*All those the Father gives me will come to me, and whoever comes to me I will never drive away. (v 37)*

Our salvation does not depend on the strength of our faith or the complete absence of doubts. Despite my wobbly faith and my faltering feelings, Jesus has got me and will not let me go. I'm not a Christian because I grew up in a Christian home in the West. I'm a Christian because God called me (just as he's calling a wonderful number of people throughout the Middle

"DESPITE MY WOBBLY FAITH AND MY FALTERING FEELINGS, JESUS HAS GOT ME AND WILL NOT LET ME GO."

#ISTHISIT

East). God is merciful—he doesn't drive me away because my faith isn't good enough. Doubt doesn't have the last word, because I've been chosen to be one of God's children—that destination is pre-determined.

Of course, there will be disciples who follow Jesus for a while and then walk away from him. Maybe that's happened to someone you know, and it's shaken your confidence. When Jesus himself stood in front of people, holding out the bread of life, "many of his disciples turned back and no longer followed him" (v 66). When that happens today, we are right to be sad—shocked, even—but we needn't be surprised.

And just because some people turn away from Christ, it doesn't mean that you will. As one friend of mine put it, the Bible's teaching on falling away can be summed up in two simple words: just don't.

## WHERE ELSE?

With many of his one-time followers turning their backs, Jesus turns to his closest friends:

> *"You do not want to leave too, do you?" Jesus asked the Twelve.*

> *Simon Peter answered him, "Lord, to whom shall we go? You have the words of eternal life. We have come to believe and to know that you are the Holy One of God." (v 67-69)*

I love the raw honesty of Peter's words here. It's a phrase that I keep coming back to when there are teachings I don't like, or feelings I can't handle, or when following Jesus just seems too hard. "To whom shall I go?" What are the alternatives? What else will satisfy?

Comparing Jesus to the alternatives is a helpful strategy against voices of scepticism. Writing for doubting non-Christians, Tim Keller says:

> "If you come to recognize the beliefs on which your doubts about Christianity are based, and if you seek as much proof for those beliefs as you seek from Christians for theirs—you will discover that your doubts are not as solid as they first appeared." (The Reason for God, page xviii)

As Christians, we too need to learn to doubt our doubts. When you hear a whisper that matter is all there is, or that prayers don't go anywhere, or that Jesus is a killjoy—challenge those doubts. What are the grounds for believing these "alternatives"? What assumptions do they rest on? And do they really satisfy?

Do this, and you'll come to the same conclusion as Peter. Jesus is not only the only option that makes sense; he's the only option full stop. We can spend the next few decades searching elsewhere for alternatives, but we won't find anything worth having. He's the only one who can give us eternal life.

## FOUR LIES SATAN LOVES TO TELL

Our doubts are not morally neutral. Ever since the Garden of Eden, Satan has been tempting God's people to disobey him by doubting his word ("Did God *really* say...?" Genesis 3 v 1). Satan was lying to Adam and Eve back then, and he's lying to you now. When we doubt, these are the lies he loves to whisper:

1. *No other Christian feels like this.* You shouldn't talk about doubt to everyone, but you do need to talk about it to someone. Choose wisely—you want to avoid rocking the faith of someone else who is struggling, so confide in someone whose

Christian maturity you respect. You might be apprehensive about how they'll react, but Jude tells Christians to "be merciful to those who doubt" (Jude v 22). Although I can't guarantee the response you'll get, I can say that I've been surprised and encouraged by the ones I've had. Ask them to pray with you and for you.

2. *You can't talk to God about this.* Like Peter, come to Jesus honestly and tell him what you're feeling—he knows anyway. The psalms are full of examples of raw, honest prayers that question why God feels far away and yet cry out to him anyway (try Psalm 13 or 42 for a start). Ask God to strengthen your faith.

3. *There's no answer to this.* If your doubts are mainly intellectual or doctrinal, then you can be sure that someone clever has already thought about it from a Christian perspective. So do a little research and poke around at the sources—you don't need to be afraid of what you might find. You'll find some places to start on page 201.

4. *Best to hit pause on your faith for a while.* The way to keep following Jesus is to keep following Jesus—to put one foot in front of the other, day by day. Keep going to church, keep reading the Bible, keep seeking to speak of Jesus to others. You'll get through this.

Ultimately, though, the best answer to Satan's lies is the resurrection. In the book of Acts, the apostles keep coming back to the fact of the resurrection as the proof that Jesus really was the Saviour sent by God that he claimed to be (for example, Acts 17 v 31).

The empty tomb is the bedrock of the Christian faith.

So when you're doubting, remind yourself of that truth and rest in it. Ask yourself: *Did Jesus rise from the dead in history?*

*Do you have any other explanation for what happened that day, and for the explosion of Christianity in the years after it? If Jesus rose from the dead, then your feelings of doubt are a lie. If he rose from the dead, what he said was true. If he rose from the dead, you can pray to him now.* Remember those two simple requirements for saving faith from Romans 10 v 9:

> *If you declare with your mouth, 'Jesus is Lord,' and believe in your heart that God raised him from the dead, you will be saved.*

Of course, all this is easier to write on a page than it is to do when you're in the throes of doubt. But don't lose hope. Days of more solid confidence are ahead...

## THE ATMOSPHERE CHANGED

A couple of years ago, I sat on a jury. In many ways it felt like being back at school. Everyone was only there because they had to be. Phones were banned. We did a lot of filing through corridors, lining up outside doors and waiting around for a group member to get back from the toilet. Worst of all, there was enforced teamwork.

The case I was on was for a robbery. As the prosecution made their case, the evidence for a guilty verdict quickly began to look convincing; we heard the witness testimony and viewed CCTV footage from right before the incident.

Then the young man who stood accused gave his defence, and things were cast into doubt. Perhaps he really was just in the wrong place with a bad crowd?

Eventually the judge summed up and we filed out to the jury deliberation room, where the enforced teamwork began. It took a few hours, but eventually the mood in the room crystallised as we settled on a unanimous verdict: the defendant was guilty. I for one was sure of it.

But it's a strange thing to have the fate of a young man in your hands—to be responsible for the direction his life will take from that moment on. It's a heavy responsibility. As we filed back into the courtroom, I began to feel nervous. What if we'd got it wrong? While the judge and the court officials went through the formalities, my sense of uncertainty grew. The foreman stood up to announce our decision. The atmosphere was tense with anticipation. I stared the defendant in the eye as the foreman declared, "We find the defendant guilty".

And with that, the atmosphere instantly changed. The tension lifted and a sudden clarity descended. The defendant shrugged—the game was up. The judge and the defence barrister discussed sentencing in a business-as-usual kind of way. What had seemed so agonisingly uncertain now seemed blindingly obvious. *Of course* he was guilty.

Here's the thing: we're living now in those moments before the verdict is delivered. We've committed to the verdict that Jesus is Lord on the basis of good evidence—but sometimes we're plagued with uncertainty. What if we've got it wrong?

But don't worry. One day, when we come before the judge of the universe, doubt will become confidence. Everything that seems in question now will become blindingly obvious. All the uncertainty will disappear and clarity will descend. *Of course* God is real.

Except that, on that day, you won't be in the jury; you'll be the accused. And the verdict for you will be different to the one the young man heard. The evidence of your sin will be stacked up against you—but Jesus will rise as your defence counsel and declare, "They're one of mine. I've already paid for the crime. Look at the evidence of the nail marks in my hands." You'll be declared "Not guilty".

I'm so looking forward to experiencing that cosmic sense of courtroom clarity. Until then—in the moments when I'm certain and in the moments when I'm not—I'll pray, in the words of the old hymn:

> *And Lord, haste the day when my faith shall be sight,*
> *The clouds be rolled back as a scroll;*
> *The trump shall resound, and the Lord shall descend,*
> *Even so, it is well with my soul.*

# 7. LONELY

## WHO ARE MY FRIENDS ANYMORE?

Lizzie had 150 guests at her wedding, and no fewer than nine bridesmaids—but when her grandad died less than a year later, she could think of no one who she wanted to call.

True friends are hard to come by. And coming by them gets harder.

As we move through our twenties, our relationships are in a state of flux as things change around us. People move away or move on—a new job, a new girlfriend or a new hobby changes the dynamics first in one relationship and then in another. Eventually most of us reach a point where we look around and ask, "Wait... where did all my friends go?"

Personally, I'm still looking for The One. By which I don't mean The Future Husband of My Dreams (although I've been searching for him too, also with limited success—more on that in Chapter Eight).

By The One, I mean my best friend. She'll be smart and funny. We'll click immediately, hang out frequently, laugh constantly, and share all our secrets and our sorrows. But there won't be too many of the latter, because life will be pretty peachy. Life with this friend will be like an episode of, well... *Friends*.

I've been looking for The One since I left school—and the search is getting more difficult the older I get. I mean, where do you meet people these days? There's church—but perhaps you find yourself feeling out of place there. You don't "fit" with the students or the families, and there aren't many others your age. There's work—but this can be hard too, depending on your job and the company culture. There are the people you live with— but if that's your family, they don't really count, and if it's shared accommodation arranged on the internet, then you're relying on pot-luck. And in my experience, the odds are long.

Then, when you do find suitable candidates to fill your "friend" vacancy, it's hard to build meaningful relationships. Time is in short supply—mainly because you've now got a job, in which you actually have to get stuff done. Repeated late nights on week-nights stop being a good idea.

But hey—at least you've still got all your old friends, right?

Or not.

These friendships are also often a struggle to maintain, especially if you're strewn across the country. Things change. You change. Over time, your circle of friends gradually boils down to just a handful of key people.

Welcome to adulthood. I told an elder at my church that I was writing this chapter, and he just looked bemused. "Isn't that how everyone feels whatever their age?" he asked. "I don't have any friends either." This isn't a phase of life—this is life.

## TWO GOLDFISH AND A BIG HANG-UP
If this is all sounding rather angsty, I should admit now that this whole area of friends is probably one of my biggest psychological hang-ups—I frequently doubt that I really have any.

I like to blame it on a relocation I took badly at the age of nine. I missed the friends I left behind so badly that I named my goldfish after them (the fish tank was an attempt by my parents to make me feel more at home). I had Esme and Diana bobbing around in the corner of my bedroom, but nine-year-old me still felt angry, alone and out of place. Only now I had a fish tank I had to clean out every week. And that's *not fun*.

Almost a couple of decades later, I'm definitely less angry (and the demise of Esme and Diana means I don't have a fish tank to clean), but I still feel alone and out of place sometimes—and it seems that feeling this way is actually pretty common. A recent study in Australia found that 67% of 18-34-year-olds felt lonely regularly or at least occasionally, with 18% saying they felt lonely every day. That's one in six of us, and double the number than among people aged 50+.

Social media means that we have more opportunities than ever to build online communities with people around the world. But far from alleviating the problem of loneliness, social media appears to actually be contributing to it. The University of Pittsburgh found that people who use social media a lot experience more social isolation than those who use it fewer than ten times a week. My guess is that you can relate to that stat. Few things fuel my loneliness more than looking on social media at people I used to know with their *other friends*.

In fact, research shows that loneliness is contagious. Chances are that you're feeling lonelier now than you did before you started the chapter, just for having read about me being lonely.

But don't stop reading now. We're about to get on to the good stuff...

# DEEP AND REAL

I've got a woeful track record when it comes to memorising passages of Scripture. I can keep them in my head for a few days or even a couple of weeks—but beyond that, passages never seem to stick.

There's one exception though: Psalm 139. I memorised it when I was far from home in a foreign country, repeating the words over and over to myself in my head. Four years later, I can still remember it because I have continued to repeat it over and over to myself in my head in those moments when I'm feeling alone. When I'm awake in my bed at 2 a.m., or driving in my car late at night, or walking someplace on my own, these are words I keep coming back to:

> *You have searched me, LORD,*
>    *and you know me.*
> *You know when I sit and when I rise;*
>    *you perceive my thoughts from afar.*
> *You discern my going out and my lying down;*
>    *you are familiar with all my ways.*
> *Before a word is on my tongue*
>    *you, LORD, know it completely.*
> *You hem me in behind and before,*
>    *and you lay your hand upon me.*
> *Such knowledge is too wonderful for me,*
>    *too lofty for me to attain. (Psalm 139 v 1-6)*

I think I'm searching for "The One"—but this psalm brings me face to face with the One I'm actually looking for. What we long for in a friend is most fulfilled when we find and truly experience relationship with God—a relationship that is deeper and more real than we have with anyone who we'd put in the category of "friend".

That's because the Lord is a God who knows you. Often at the heart of loneliness is a desire to be known, wholly and completely. But my church friends don't know anything about who I was before I was 21. My school friends know the history that has shaped me, but have little idea about what drives me day to day now. My work colleagues see a lot of me day by day, but they don't really know what I did at the weekend. My whole life feels segmented. No one knows the whole 360 degrees of my existence. Except, that is, God.

God knows "when I sit and when I rise ... my going out and my lying down".

God knows that I went to spin class yesterday.

God knows how well I slept last night.

God knows that I really need to buy toothpaste this afternoon, what I'm loving on Netflix at the moment, and what I'm doing on Saturday.

God is "familiar with all my ways".

He knows, he knows, he knows all 360 degrees of you. He knows you even better than you know yourself.

It actually starts to feel a bit unsettling. At the same time as wanting a friend who knows us and gets us, we actually also fear being truly known. We don't want people to see our flaws and our weaknesses and all the embarrassing things we think and feel. That's why I'm terrified by the mere thought of you reading this right now and forming an opinion of me.

Yet God sees further still. He doesn't just observe my diary from a distance; he sees the inside of me too: "You perceive my thoughts from afar ... Before a word is on my tongue you, LORD, know it completely" (v 2, 4). He knows who I'm jealous of. He knows who I look down on. He knows about the ugly pride I do my best to cover up.

But in God we find what no friend would ever be—someone who is with us and for us, in spite of knowing us completely. He looks at our darker parts and loves us anyway, instead of walking away in disappointment or disgust.

## THROUGH THICK AND THIN

God doesn't just know you—he *acts for you*:

> *Where can I go from your Spirit?*
>   *Where can I flee from your presence?*
> *If I go up to the heavens, you are there;*
>   *if I make my bed in the depths, you are there.*
> *If I rise on the wings of the dawn,*
>   *if I settle on the far side of the sea,*
> *even there your hand will guide me,*
>   *your right hand will hold me fast.*
> *If I say, "Surely the darkness will hide me*
>   *and the light become night around me,"*
> *even the darkness will not be dark to you;*
>   *the night will shine like the day,*
>   *for darkness is as light to you. (v 7-12)*

God sticks with us through thick and thin. It's impossible to go long-distance with God because he's literally everywhere—even on "the far side of the sea".

These verses hint at spiritual distance, as well as geographical distance. God is there in those moments when we feel sublimely close to him. But he's equally there when we deliberately pull away from him—in those times when we make our metaphorical beds in stupid places and stubbornly insist on lying in them. He sees every ugly thought and unkind word—and still he doesn't let go of us. He's there even when our circumstances are so bleak that we've lost all hope.

And what is it that he's doing? He's both guiding you forward and holding you fast. He's like a parent with a toddler who's unsteady on their feet, his hand firmly gripping yours so that you don't topple over.

We relish the warmth and familiarity of old friendships— those relationships that seem to fit us just right, like an old sweater that smells of home, knitted together with the threads of shared memories. You and God go way back like that—and you'll go way onwards too...

> *For you created my inmost being;*
>    *you knit me together in my mother's womb.*
> *I praise you because I am fearfully and wonderfully made;*
>    *your works are wonderful,*
>    *I know that full well.*
> *My frame was not hidden from you*
>    *when I was made in the secret place,*
>    *when I was woven together in the depths of the earth.*
> *Your eyes saw my unformed body;*
>    *all the days ordained for me were written in your book*
>    *before one of them came to be.*
> *How precious to me are your thoughts, God!*
>    *How vast is the sum of them!*
> *Were I to count them,*
>    *they would outnumber the grains of sand—*
>    *when I awake, I am still with you. (v 13-18)*

Whether we're feeling lonely or not, verse 16 is a Quarter-Life-Crisis-busting truth. "All the days ordained for me were written in your book before one of them came to be." Just think of that for a moment: the boring ones and the fun ones—they're all there. All the days ahead of you, and all the days behind you—all written down. The ones you've forgotten, as well as the ones that you wish you could forget. The ones where you wake up happy and go to bed sad, and where you wake up sad and go to bed happy.

So if I'm longing for someone to just tell this stuff to—someone who would just listen long enough or care deeply enough—I can look to God and know that I've found that someone. You might have heard Christianity described as "a personal relationship with God". The trouble is often that we don't treat it like it's that personal. I look at David's words in this psalm and struggle to relate them to my own "walk with the Lord". But if we're trusting in Christ, a relationship with God that is this personal *has been* opened up to us. Christ's death provides "a new and living way opened for us" into God's presence, which means that we can "draw near to God" himself (Hebrews 10 v 20-22).

If your relationship with God doesn't *feel* that personal at the moment, know that it *can* feel like that:

> *Search me, God, and know my heart;*
> *test me and know my anxious thoughts.*
> *See if there is any offensive way in me,*
> *and lead me in the way everlasting. (Psalm 139 v 23-24)*

Searching, knowing, testing, seeing, leading—this is the way that God related to David, and this is the way that God relates to us as we read and remember his word.

Often I get that list wrong—I approach the Bible as if it's all about me reading, understanding, thinking, knowing. Which it is, a bit. But if those were the terms on which I approached a human friendship, things would flounder pretty quickly (partly because you'd think I was a bit weird and intense).

When we read God's word, we're coming to listen to a living God who is speaking to us—not as a politician does through a TV screen but as a friend does face to face. Scripture is brought alive to us by the Spirit in a way which means that as we read it, God is searching us, knowing us, testing us, seeing us and leading us.

In his book *You Can Really Grow*, John Hindley makes the point that we are meant to read the Bible not as an instruction manual or a tick-box exercise but as a love letter:

> "The Bible is first and foremost a love letter, from Christ, to his people. ... It will change so much ... if you sit down with your Bible, ask the Spirit for help, and think: I am about to hear from Jesus, about Jesus. I am opening up his love letter. He is true, he is beautiful, and he is speaking to me."
>
> *(pages 56, 66)*

Open the Bible with this expectation, and God will stir your heart and your thoughts, and guide you step by step closer to glory.

If you're a 20-something lamenting your lack of friends, lean on this One. And know this: you are not alone.

## SIX BITS OF NO-NONSENSE FRIENDSHIP ADVICE

Knowing God in this way frees us from approaching other people as a means of meeting our own emotional needs, and liberates us to seek to meet theirs.

The irony is that the more we embrace this personal relationship with God, the more we're freed to enjoy our friendships.

We won't use other people as a tool to make ourselves feel good. We won't burden them with expectations they cannot meet. We'll be free to simply love others, commit to others and tell the truth to others—without always worrying about what they'll think, or whether we'd be having more fun hanging out with someone else.

As we approach life in this way we'll find that, more often than not, we get good friends by being a good friend. After all, God intends for us to enjoy quality human friendships—"it is not good for the man to be alone" (Genesis 2 v 18).

But what exactly does it look like to be a good friend? Let's turn to Proverbs for six pieces of no-nonsense practical advice.

## 1. QUALITY, NOT QUANTITY

*One who has unreliable friends soon comes to ruin, but there is a friend who sticks closer than a brother.*

*(Proverbs 18 v 24)*

Sometimes I look at people with more friends and busier social lives and feel... well, jealous. But Proverbs reminds us that it is the quality of relationships, not the quantity, that really matters. Your loneliness will not be eased by amassing a network of unreliable or distant "friends" or well-meaning acquaintances, or trying to keep up with every single person you've ever been friends with. It's far better (and a lot less exhausting) to cultivate the kind of relationships where you stick by each other like family. That takes time.

In this, there is a place for intentionality. Seek out relationships with those you know who have the godliness to be a close friend, and the personality to be *your* close friend. Take the initiative in growing those friendships. Don't anoint one particular acquaintance as The (Future) One, and then grow despondent and bitter when things don't work out that way. Equally, don't worry about how many friends someone already has, as though that automatically means there's no room for friendship with you. No one's ranking their Top 8 Friends on MySpace anymore like it's 2006. We're grown-ups.

## 2. INVEST WHERE YOU ARE

*Do not go to your relative's house when disaster strikes*
*you—better a neighbour nearby than a relative far away.*

*(27 v 10)*

If we—or our friends—have relocated, it's tempting to think of our Real Friends as those who are far away. We might spend our evenings calling them, and our weekends driving to see them. There's nothing inherently wrong with this—but there is a danger that we fail to make time to build relationships where we actually are. You don't just need Christian friends (although you certainly don't need *only* Christian friends, either)—you need Christian friends *at your church*, who you see once a week or more. They don't need to be like you—a similar age or stage or background—they just have to be "neighbours": they just have to be nearby.

There's an emotional element to this too. If I'm depending emotionally on people far away, I won't need to depend emotionally on people who are nearby—and that emotional interconnectedness is essential to real friendship.

So where are you investing? Who are you depending on? Are they nearby or far away?

## 3. LOVE AT ALL TIMES

*A friend loves at all times, and a brother is born for a time of*
*adversity. (17 v 17)*

This one's easy to write, but harder to live: just keep loving. Love people when life is fun and easy, and when life is boring or hard. And remember that your friendships will feel more meaningful the more of the magic ingredient you add: time.

When we do friendship on autopilot, we'll quickly surround ourselves with friends who are like us or make ourselves feel good. But we need to be ready to come alongside brothers and sisters who are facing more than their fair share of adversity. That's what God has made you family for.

## 4. FORGIVE FREELY

*Whoever would foster love covers over an offence, but whoever repeats the matter separates close friends. (17 v 9)*

The closer you get to someone, the more opportunities you will have to annoy each other. But under normal circumstances, this isn't a reason to pull back and move on—it's an opportunity to love in a way that is truly Christ-like, by "covering over" the offence. This means having an attitude that says, *What you did or said hurt me, but I'm going to bear the emotional cost and choose to keep loving you. I'm not going to gossip about you or complain about you to other people.*

And of course, often you'll be the one who needs to say sorry. One of the things that has actually deepened my relationships most is the act of apologising and receiving forgiveness—usually after I've said something stupid. Be quick to say sorry.

## 5. SPEAK GRACE

*One who loves a pure heart and who speaks with grace will have the king for a friend. (22 v 11)*

We often think "good conversation" is when it flows naturally and easily. But truly good conversation is speaking with grace.

Part of this is speaking *of* grace—reminding one another that what God has given to us is far in excess of anything that we deserve. But we're also to seek to speak *with* grace, filling our conversations with words that are true, kind, gentle, joyful, grateful and loving. Christian "banter" is fun at best, hurtful at worst, and most of the time just unproductive. People who speak with grace are a true joy to be around.

If you're anything like me, this doesn't come easily—but God's Spirit can help us. So when you're on your way to church or to meet up with someone, take a moment to pray, "Lord, please give me an opportunity to speak grace to this person today".

### 6. BE VULNERABLE
*Perfume and incense bring joy to the heart, and the*
*pleasantness of a friend springs from their heartfelt advice.*
(27 v 9)

*Vulnerable.* I hate that word—first, because it's clichéd, and second, because it's uncomfortable. But joy in relationships comes from a heartfelt exchange—and for that to happen, someone's got to start.

So here's a challenge for the next time you're with someone you know a bit, or in a Bible study: just say something honest about yourself. "I'm feeling..." or "I'm struggling with..." Push past the fear of awkwardness, and persevere in seeking to be honest even if it doesn't get the results you want immediately. Bare your heart a bit, and you might just get the joy of some heartfelt advice back.

## PROVIDE WHO I NEED
Earlier, I said that the area of friendship is one of my biggest psychological hang-ups—but as I look back over the past year

it's also one of the areas where I have seen God's goodness to me most clearly. A while back I was haemorrhaging friends at an alarming rate. They kept getting married, or moving away, or both. I keep a journal (it's kind of like this book, but even more self-absorbed), and in a rare moment of spiritual maturity I wrote that I was "trusting God to provide who I need for the next season".

And he has. He's put new people across my path. He's given me opportunities to grow acquaintances into something deeper. I still feel lonely sometimes, but less so than I have in the past.

Friendships don't happen instantly. If you're still pining for The One, let me break it to you: they probably aren't out there. Adult relationships just don't tend to work that way.

But God can and will provide you with what you need and who you need. Supremely, of course, he has provided you with himself. So turn to the One who knows you and loves you, and ask him to provide the human friendships you'd like. You might just be surprised by the way that he answers.

# 8. SINGLE

## WHY ARE ALL MY FRIENDS GETTING MARRIED?

Before we begin, some context: my sister is getting married in eleven days' time.

In case you're not one of two sisters, you should know that they spend a large part of their childhood being jealous of each other. She: beautiful and charismatic. Me: clever and generally well-behaved. (You can tell who I'd rather be, right?) But now we're grown-ups with our own separate lives, neither of us feels like we live in the other one's shadow. Instead, we can shine a light on the ways that the other one sparkles.

And on her wedding day, Martha sure will sparkle.

Yet the truth is... I want it to be me.

Don't get me wrong—I love my sister and I'm very much looking forward to celebrating with her. But at the same time, part of me is dreading the family photos with my siblings all lined up with their partners and me on my own. Of all the weddings I've been to, this one will take me closest to seeing what the look on my father's face would be if he ever walks me down the aisle. And all the while I'll be knowing it isn't me; and all the while I'll be suspecting that it never will be.

Why am I telling you all this? Because I want you to know that I'm writing this chapter needing and wanting the things I'm about to write to be true—perhaps now more than ever.

Actually, this is a chapter that you need to read, wherever you're "at". Yes, it's for you if you're single—whether it turns out to be just for now or for a lifetime. (And maybe you know that it will almost certainly be a lifetime, because you're same-sex-attracted and can't assume that marriage will ever be an option for you).

But this chapter is also for you if you're dating, engaged or married. For one thing, you may well end up single again one day. (Or perhaps that's you already, and now you feel like you don't fit into anyone's box.) And for another, whatever your relationship status, you'll definitely have single friends who need you to speak helpful truths to them, rather than thoughtless remarks, hurtful banter or useless platitudes.

In some ways I suspect that I'm a little young to be writing on singleness (or, truth be told, on anything much at all…). What I'm about to write doesn't come with the tested resilience of a man or woman in their 40s or 50s who's spent decades being single. I've still got it pretty easy in many ways—a lot of my friends are unattached (although the number shrinks year on year), and almost none of them have children yet.

If you're single, I expect that your feelings about that "status" have changed a fair bit over the last ten years. Maybe the ticking of your biological clock is increasing its volume over time—and your sense of panic or sadness rises with it. Or as one friend who is in their late twenties recently observed, "At first, all my Christian friends got married, and I didn't. And now all my non-Christian friends are getting married too. I've felt out of sync with one cohort for ages. Now I feel out of sync with both." This friend said the most helpful thing they've found in coming to terms with their own prolonged singleness is seeing it as a sort of grieving process—mourning the increasingly probable loss of the life they'd always hoped for, and coming to accept how things are likely to be instead.

You might have heard of the "Five stages of grief" set out by the psychologist Elisabeth Kübler-Ross. Here's how that looks for Christians when it comes to unwanted singleness:

- Denial: *This cannot possibly be it. I'll find someone one day. I'm only __ years old. I've got loads of time.*

- Anger: *Why would God withhold this from me? It's not fair. I would be a much better boy/girlfriend than him/her. How can it be right that they've got someone and I haven't?*

- Bargaining: *God, what do you want from me? I've been serving loads in church, and reading my Bible, and still nothing on the relationship front. Maybe it's true what they say—it's when you stop looking that you find someone. Maybe if I was more _____ , then that person would like me.*

- Depression: *No one wants me. I'll always be alone.* *Crying face emoji*

And perhaps, for some of us...

- Acceptance: *Maybe I won't ever get married. And maybe that's OK. And maybe it's even OK that it's OK.*

I don't know where you fall on that scale. I reckon it must be possible to go backwards and forwards because I'm pretty sure

I have. But for many, the Quarter-Life Crisis really comes to a crunch when we realise that we may well end up doing the next three-quarters of life on our own. If that thought fills you with dread, keep reading.

## HOW TO BE OK TODAY

You might have already read and heard a lot on singleness before. You've heard about the gift of singleness—and rolled your eyes at all the jokes about it being the gift everyone wants to return. You've spoken to people who talk about being content with their singleness—but can't imagine that ever being you. You've thrown yourself into church or work or sports or whatever—but it hasn't helped with your loneliness. You know all the right answers—but answers don't give you the human touch that you crave.

The truth is, you just didn't expect to be this age and still not engaged or married, or enjoying the kind of serious relationship that allows you to dream with realism. Now you can't shake the feeling that you're running out of time (not to mention eligible options). You're starting to panic: *What if I never get married? What if I'm single for ever?*

That's why I want to start this chapter in the book of Lamentations. I know what you're thinking: "Lamentations?! I thought you were trying to make me feel better about being single, not worse?" But bear with me:

> Because of the LORD's great love we are not consumed,
>     for his compassions never fail.
> They are new every morning;
>     great is your faithfulness.
> I say to myself, "The LORD is my portion;
>     therefore I will wait for him." (Lamentations 3 v 22-24)

This is helpful for two reasons. First, if right now you're feeling unloved, unchosen and undesirable, know that God loves you greatly. He chose you to be part of his people, and he wanted that enough to send his Son to save you from being consumed by the anger you're due.

And second, the Lord's compassions are new every morning.

That means that right now, you don't need to be OK with being single in fifty years' time. You don't need to look with dread down the timeline to the season when all your friends have kids (and then grandkids). You don't need to panic about what you'll do financially, or where you'll spend your holidays, or who will choose your care home. The Lord's compassions are new every morning. Contentment with our singleness isn't a status that we arrive at and then bask in for the rest of our lives. It's something we depend on the Lord to give us each day.

So here's the key question: is there a way to be OK with being single *today*? Not with still being single tomorrow, or next Christmas, or when you're 30 or 40—but just *today*.

We're about to look at some good reasons why you can be OK. But before we get to those, remember that *today* is what matters. Because if you can be OK being single today, you can be OK being single tomorrow when it becomes today, and the day after that, and all the days that follow. Why? Because God's compassions are new every morning—he will be tomorrow all that you need him to be. In 30 years' time, he will be faithful. In 50 years' time, he will not fail you. Perhaps you will get married (and you'll wish you spent less time in your single years worrying about it) or maybe you won't. Either way, God will prove himself faithful—day after day after day.

So can you be OK being single today? Yes, you can be. And here's why.

## SINGLE IS GOOD (YES, BUT...)

The Bible passage you're about to read is pretty radical. My pastor preached on it at our church recently, and at the end of the service there was an anonymous Q&A text-in. In effect, the questions almost all started with "Yes, but..." People just couldn't get their heads round the idea that the apostle Paul actually means what he says here. But he does. So spend some time taking it in for yourself:

> [25]*Now about virgins: I have no command from the Lord, but I give a judgment as one who by the Lord's mercy is trustworthy.* [26]*Because of the present crisis, I think that it is good for a man to remain as he is.* [27]*Are you pledged to a woman? Do not seek to be released. Are you free from such a commitment? Do not look for a wife.* [28]*But if you do marry, you have not sinned; and if a virgin marries, she has not sinned. But those who marry will face many troubles in this life, and I want to spare you this.*
>
> [29]*What I mean, brothers and sisters, is that the time is short. From now on those who have wives should live as if they do not;* [30]*those who mourn, as if they did not; those who are happy, as if they were not; those who buy something, as if it were not theirs to keep;* [31]*those who use the things of the world, as if not engrossed in them. For this world in its present form is passing away.*
>
> [32]*I would like you to be free from concern. An unmarried man is concerned about the Lord's affairs—how he can please the Lord.* [33]*But a married man is concerned about the affairs of this world—how he can please his wife—*[34]*and his interests*

*are divided. An unmarried woman or virgin is concerned about the Lord's affairs: her aim is to be devoted to the Lord in both body and spirit. But a married woman is concerned about the affairs of this world—how she can please her husband. [35]I am saying this for your own good, not to restrict you, but that you may live in a right way in undivided devotion to the Lord.*

*[36]If anyone is worried that he might not be acting honourably towards the virgin he is engaged to, and if his passions are too strong and he feels he ought to marry, he should do as he wants. He is not sinning. They should get married. [37]But the man who has settled the matter in his own mind, who is under no compulsion but has control over his own will, and who has made up his mind not to marry the virgin—this man also does the right thing. [38]So then, he who marries the virgin does right, but he who does not marry her does better. (1 Corinthians 7 v 25-38)*

By "virgins", Paul means those who are not, and have never been, married.

(And it's worth saying that whatever has happened in your romantic history, if you're not married then this passage applies equally to you—God's grace gives all of us a clean slate. While you may bear emotional scars from past mistakes, God's not punishing you for them, and he's not defining you by them, and you don't need to either.)

In this part of the letter, Paul's doing his own sort of Q&A in response to the questions the Christians in Corinth have asked him. The question here is, essentially, *Hey Paul, sex is bad, right? It's all a bit dirty, not very spiritual, and best avoided.* Or in their own words, "It is good for a man not to have sexual relations with a woman" (v 1).

In the first half of the chapter Paul says that sex within marriage is not bad, and that husbands and wives should be committed to one another physically, both seeking to be selfless with their bodies. But then in our passage, he goes on to explain what else is "good": not getting married at all (v 26).

This is not meant to undervalue marriage. Paul stresses several times that getting married is not sinful (v 28, 36)—it's a gift from God (v 7). *If you want to get married,* says Paul, *be my guest.* (Or rather, *I'll be your guest.*) If you long to be married, and you're looking to get married, that's OK—it's not a sign of sin and it's certainly not a sign of weakness. Marriage is good. Parenthood is good. On one level, it's good to want both of these things.

But verse 38 sums up Paul's radical argument: *married-and-sexually-active is good... but single-and-celibate is better.*

And that's something that we find very hard to believe—especially in our sex-obsessed Western culture, and especially in our marriage-obsessed *church* culture.

So what would it take for you and me to think that Paul is right? What does he see that we don't?

I reckon that, for most of us, what we're missing is not some insight that Paul has on the states of marriage and singleness themselves. No—what we're missing is Paul's perspective on time. The reason it's good to remain single is "because of the present crisis" (v 26). Paul clarifies what this "crisis" is a few verses later: "What I mean, brothers and sisters, is that the time is short ... For this world in its present form is passing away" (v 29, 31).

This world is on borrowed time. A day is coming when Christ is going to return and renew creation completely. That means that although we continue now to take an active part in "the things of this world"—getting and being married, earning and spending money, grieving losses and celebrating victories—we do so knowing that none of those things are what matters most, because none of those things will last (v 29-31). One day our spouses won't be our spouses, our earthly joys and sorrows will not define us, and nothing we owned will be ours to keep (see Luke 20 v 34-36). And that day is coming soon.

Until then, the one thing that matters is making sure that we are ready for it—and helping others to be ready for it too. If you knew that the world was going to end tonight, you probably wouldn't spend your final hours swiping right on Tinder.

The best thing we can do with the hours—or years—we have left until the Lord returns is to live wholeheartedly for him. And Paul's logic is that being single puts us in a better position to do that. *This is the urgent, all-consuming reality we're in,* Paul says, *so why would you want to be anything but single?*

After all, a married person has their interests "divided". There's no denying that a spouse (and children) brings demands on someone's time and money. Schedules have to be planned with them in mind. Decisions have to take them into account.

You've probably come across the commonly-held myth that single people have more time than married people. It's not true. God gives us all 24 hours in a day and seven days in a week. But as a single person, I do have a greater degree of flexibility in how I use those 24 hours. While I do have responsibilities, they are not the kind that need to be put to bed at 7:30 p.m. every night. By and large, I can eat when I want in the evening, go where I want at the weekend, and tidy my room only when I deem it necessary.

This gives me incredible flexibility in working for "the Lord's affairs". I can meet up with someone one-to-one. I can take up an obscure hobby in order to meet new people in the community. I can offer to lead a Bible study next week. I can spend a week of my summer volunteering on a Christian camp. I can move house to be part of a church plant. I can even babysit for my married friends...

## DON'T WASTE IT – USE IT

So ask yourself: is Paul's summary of the single life an accurate summary of how you're using yours? How would you finish off verse 32 or 34 if it was about you? "An unmarried man/woman [who] is concerned about..." Getting married? Buying a house? Advancing her career? Travelling the world on his motorbike? Or "the Lord's affairs"?

If I'm honest, most of the time "the Lord's affairs" are pretty far down the list of my concerns. I'm out to please myself, not Jesus. I'm devoted to my own comfort, not the Lord's agenda. Which means that I rejoice in my singleness only so far as it serves those priorities. In moments when I reckon I'd be more comfortable or more happy with a partner, contentment becomes impossible—because it's comfort or happiness that I ultimately want, not "to please the Lord". When that happens, I view my singleness as a hindrance to my happiness, not as a gift for my good. My singleness can only be a good thing if my life's aim is to be "devoted to the Lord": 100% invested in living for him. When I'm discontent with my singleness, it's usually because my priorities have gone awry.

So what would it look like for you to live more like the unmarried man or woman of verse 32 or 34? This isn't a question of schedule—it's a question of attitude. Here you are, in the prime of your life, free to use your time and energy on the things that matter. Don't waste your singleness. Use it.

But this passage also puts paid to the myth that if we're single we're somehow lacking something. After all, if I don't have another half (or a "better half", *vomit*), then, well... I'm only a half. Not so, says Paul. In fact, in these verses it is married people who are "divided", not single people. The unmarried person is free to be "devoted to the Lord in both body and spirit"—that's a description of wholeness, not half-ness. The sense of completeness that we long for will not come from getting married and having our interests divid-ed—it will come from living more wholeheartedly for Jesus. And knowing this and clinging to this is what will keep me, and you, from a growing bitterness in our hearts, and from going out with someone who cannot help us with the Lord's affairs because they don't know or love the Lord at all (1 Cor-inthians 7 v 39; 2 Corinthians 6 v 14-18).

It's only in Jesus that we will have our deepest aches and long-ings fulfilled. Completely.

## WHEN JESUS CAN'T EMPTY YOUR MOUSE TRAPS

And all that's great... in theory. But it doesn't appear to help you with your lust, or your loneliness. It doesn't seem to make turning up to social events alone any easier. It won't do much to help you make life decisions on your own. It doesn't seem to make your sexual desires go away. As one friend with a rodent problem in her house told me, "I get that Jesus is everything, but he's not here physically—it's a physical relationship that I crave more than anything else. Plus, Jesus can't empty my mouse traps." (Because it's hard to stay a feminist when it comes to dealing with dead rodents.)

Life as a single Christian just seems so... hard.

You're not the first to think that. In fact, there's an incident in Luke's Gospel where the disciples are dismayed at how hard following Jesus seems.

> *Peter said to him, "We have left all we had to follow you!"*
>
> *"Truly I tell you," Jesus said to them, "no one who has left home or wife or brothers or sisters or parents or children for the sake of the kingdom of God will fail to receive many times as much in this age, and in the age to come eternal life." (Luke 18 v 28-30)*

Jesus' words show that church is meant to be family—it's the place where we find brothers and sisters and parents and children and home. When you get the dreaded question, "Do you have a family?" in a very real sense the answer is "yes"— you do have a family. You're part of the family of God. If you need someone to empty your mousetraps, you should be able to find that person in the church. (Or buy a pair of gloves and watch some YouTube tutorials so that you can empty other people's mousetraps.) There ought to be no lonely people in God's family.

And yet sometimes our churches aren't all that we want them or need them to be. Often church is the hardest place to be single, when really it should be the easiest. Some people say the stupidest things. When I started writing this chapter, I was sure I was going to include a list of all the cutting or careless remarks that anyone has ever made to me about being single. Maybe you carry a similar list around in your head.

But I haven't written that list. Because truthfully, I've said cutting and careless things on nearly every subject under the sun—and there are definitely people who have gone lonely on my watch. While there's certainly a place to lovingly challenge (married) people to live up to Jesus' vision of the church family, harbouring bitterness or feeling sorry for myself won't do much to help. Showing grace beats playing the victim every time. So if you think no one ever invites you round for dinner because you don't have a partner, invite them round for dinner and show them it works.

Sometimes we will have to work harder than we ought to in order to create community. But we can still try to be grateful for the little things. There's a guy in my small group called Ieuan who changes the light bulbs in my car and helps me move house with his van. I'm grateful for a brother in Christ like him. I have a friend called Claire who has me around for dinner before the church prayer meeting, and lets me play with her crazy kids before bedtime. I'm grateful for a sister in Christ like her. There are little souls that I get to watch grow into big personalities week by week and year by year. I'm grateful for children in Christ like that. God has given me plenty of little people to treasure, even if I never have children of my own.

Whatever your church is like, I'm guessing you've got people you can be grateful for too.

## DON'T BE CONTENT BEING SINGLE

Earlier in this chapter I asked, *Is there a way to be OK with being single today?*

Well, there is. And yet the truth is, contentment with our singleness isn't really the aim.

I don't need to seek to be more content with my singleness—not today, not on my sister's wedding day, not ever, really. Instead, I need to be more convinced that "this world in its present form is passing away" (1 Corinthians 7 v 31). I need to be so consumed with this coming reality that whether I'm single or married just doesn't matter that much. I need to lift my eyes to a different horizon—beyond the what-ifs and if-onlys of the next few decades—to the awesome certainty that is thundering towards me.

Because even the best marriage is only ever a picture of what lies ahead for every Christian. The permanent relationship of love and intimacy between a husband and wife—the relationship that perhaps even now your heart aches for—is a little preview of your future. It points to a time when the bride of Christ, the church, is brought to meet her groom and enjoy a truly permanent relationship of love and intimacy with him. Marriage is only ever the trailer. Being single now is like missing the three-minute trailer for an epic film that you're going to end up seeing the whole three hours of anyway.

On that wedding day in heaven, no Christian will feel like they've missed out or have been left out. This world and all its relationships in their present form are passing away. Why would I spend my 20s pining for a day that may or may not happen, when I can instead spend them preparing for a day that definitely will?

Here's what I need to do to prepare for my sister's wedding. Here's what you and I need to do to prepare for every wedding we go to. In fact, here's what we essentially need to do every day to help us prepare for that great heavenly wedding of our own.

In eleven days' time I'll wake up early. I'll read the Bible. I'll remind myself just how much God loves me and how much Christ gave up for me and gave to me. I'll remember that God has especially chosen me to be part of his bride—not because

"WE NEED TO LIFT OUR
EYES TO A DIFFERENT
HORIZON — BEYOND
THE WHAT-IFS AND
IF-ONLYS OF THE NEXT
FEW DECADES."

#ISTHISIT

I'm desirable, but just because he loves me. And then I'll talk to him. I'll pray for the bride and groom and ask God to be gracious to them in the years ahead. I'll think over the day in front of me, and I'll ask God to use one person I talk to to encourage me that day. And I'll ask him to use me to encourage one person as well—for an opportunity to speak the name of Jesus with a huge smile on my face.

And you know what? I'm pretty sure he'll answer.

# 9. DATING & MARRIAGE
## IS THIS NORMAL OR HAVE I MADE A HUGE MISTAKE?

Despite having never been married, I am well accustomed to giving marriage advice.

At this stage of life, you tend to get invited to a lot of weddings—and often to the "pre-wedding" too. Call it what you like—bridal showers or hen parties or stag do's or bachelor parties—they're all names for the celebration in honour of the celebration.

One thing that marks out the showers from the stags (and the girls from the guys) is that, at least in my experience, the bride-to-be's guests are invariably asked to provide a piece of marriage advice for some cute scrapbook or silly game.

Having been caught unprepared many times, I have found a stock piece of marriage advice to hang onto. I dispense it when invited to at any occasion—and occasionally when uninvited too. (Maybe I'd be invited to more occasions if I didn't.) It's this:

*Remember there's more than one way to stack a dishwasher.*

I read this line in a newspaper once and it seemed to make sense, so I have repeated it to others. I've taken the same approach to writing this chapter.

I've listened to what people have told me about marriage and dating relationships, and whatever seemed biblical, useful and wise, I am repeating. But I'll admit that a lot of this is beyond the limits of my own experience. The last time I felt my heart beat, my stomach churn and my knees weaken was last Monday at spin class.

I like the dishwasher advice because poorly stacked dishwashers are one of my greatest frustrations in life; and if I ever get married, I imagine it could quickly turn into a source of strife. The line works on a literal level—but also on a metaphorical one. When two people build a life together, they quickly discover that there's more than one way to do most things. And their partner normally has a different way. Most couples have to learn the give-and-take of compromise.

Relationships are as wonderfully diverse as the different people who form them. That means that hard-and-fast rules from a book aren't particularly helpful. Much like dishwasher stacking, there's more than one way to do dating, and there's more than one way to do marriage.

That said, when it comes to dishwashers, there are a few red lines. My friend Helen told me that my trusty line was, in fact, stupid and wrong—because "Jack puts the bowls in the dishwasher face up, so they fill with scummy water. That's not OK. That's just wrong." Likewise, Scripture gives us some red lines when it comes to our relationships. But on the whole, it gives principles—how they work out in practice is actually pretty flexible.

## BEYOND "LOVE IS KIND..."

I guess you'd be hard-pressed to find a spouse who has at no stage looked at their marriage and thought, "Is this it? I thought it would go better/feel easier than this." Reality doesn't always live up to expectations.

When it comes to picking a reading for their wedding, most couples go with something nice like 1 Corinthians 13. But after a few months or years of marriage, maybe things are starting to look less patient-and-kind, and more James 4:

> *What causes fights and quarrels among you? Don't they come from your desires that battle within you? You desire but do not have, so you kill. You covet but you cannot get what you want, so you quarrel and fight. You do not have because you do not ask God. When you ask, you do not receive, because you ask with wrong motives, that you may spend what you get on your pleasures. (James 4 v 1-3)*

OK, that's extreme. In fact, the "kill" James speaks about is likely metaphorical. (Although, this seems an apt place to say that domestic abuse does happen, and if that's your situation then please ignore this chapter, get yourself and any dependants you have out of danger, and get help.) But I admired one friend's honesty when she admitted:

> *"Before I got married, I had never been so angry that I couldn't speak. But that's what happened on my honeymoon. My husband said something that made me so angry that I couldn't get any words out. Then he ended up crying because he could see how much he'd upset me. It was a mess."*

James is actually talking to a church community here, not a couple—but the same principles apply. So how would you answer James' question? What causes fights and quarrels (and strongly worded disagreements and resentful remarks and all usage of the silent treatment) in your marriage?

Your instinct is probably to point to someone else as the problem—namely, your spouse (or your in-laws). But James puts the responsibility for conflict somewhere else: it comes "from your desires that battle within you". As Sam Allberry puts it, "Conflict comes because our own selfish desires are not being met" (*James For You*, p 106).

So we can't grow any relationship by trying to fix the other person, or by changing our circumstances—because that's not the main cause of our problems. We need to look at our own hearts first...

## WHEN YOU'RE FOUND IN THE WRONG BED

In the next verses, James changes tack and starts talking about a different "couple":

> *You adulterous people, don't you know that friendship with the world means enmity against God? Therefore, anyone who chooses to be a friend of the world becomes an enemy of God. Or do you think Scripture says without reason that he jealously longs for the spirit he has caused to dwell in us? (v 4-5)*

Throughout the Bible, God speaks about his relationship with his people in terms of a marriage. In fact, that's the reason why, for all the moments of pressure, marriage is great. It's been designed as a snapshot of something awesome—the relationship between Christ and his church (Ephesians 5 v 25-32). If the panoramic picture is of Jesus and his people, it makes sense that even the thumbnail image of earthly marriage is, on balance, really very good.

But for James' readers, there's a problem: God has caught them in bed with the world. Embracing the values of the world—that attitude that rejects God's authority and ultimately puts self first—is cheating on God. We can't be wholeheartedly committed to loving him while loving the world at the same time. Often being married shows us just how much we love what we want and how naturally we live for ourselves.

James describes God as a husband who is justly angry at his wife's unfaithfulness. Yet despite our betrayal, he wants us back. He "jealously longs" for us.

So what does he do? *We* are spiritually adulterous...

> But **he** gives us more grace. That is why Scripture says:
> "God opposes the proud
>    but shows favour to the humble."
>
> *(James 4 v 6, my emphasis)*

In the face of our selfishness, God gives us more grace. In spite of our sin, God gives us more grace. When we run after anything and everything but the Giver of all good things, God gives us more grace. He continues to give more second chances, more generous gifts, more of his Spirit to help us keep going. He neither gives up nor gives way—he gives grace.

This, in six words, is the gospel: "But he gives us more grace". These words define your relationship with your heavenly Father today. And these words can—and should—define your marriage.

How? Here are six points to start with:

### 1. FORGIVE QUICKLY
"Love is only a feeling," sang an obscure British rock band back in the 00s. But the Bible says that love is more than a feeling—

it's a decision. It's something someone chooses to express. And that's a good thing, because it means that when God looks at our unloveliness, he chooses to love and forgive us anyway. He gives us more grace.

When you look at your spouse, that is what they need too— even in those moments when you don't "feel" loving towards them because they're not, frankly, being particularly love-able.

So often, we want to win the argument just for the sake of it. Or we stubbornly pitch our tent on the moral high ground, and sit shivering on the top of the mountain while looking with disdain at the person below. Or we hold on to a grudge, ready to bring up a past mistake when we next need to prove a point or win a row.

But God gives more grace—and so must we. Be quick to say "I forgive you" when you need to. Be quick to say "I'm sorry" when you need to. Neither is easy to say and mean—both are necessary when two sinners live together. If we remember how much and how often God gives us more grace, we'll be empowered to show grace to others.

## 2. ALLOW YOURSELF TO BE HUMBLED

One common theme comes out when I chat to people about their marriages: being married is a humbling experience. It seems like bringing another person's sin into the mix stirs the pot so that yours bubbles to the surface in more obvious ways than ever before.

But when that happens, you're right where God wants you to be. "God opposes the proud"—those who think they're OK really— and "gives grace to the humble" (v 6, ESV)—those who acknowledge what a mess their heart is. So let marriage humble you. Don't try to gloss over the issues or think that if you just try a little harder it will be alright. If you need to seek some outside help for your marriage, that's not a sign of failure but of humility. It's when you feel weak that God shows you favour.

One of the ways God shows us his favour is by making us more like Christ. And ultimately, daily seeking to grow more like Jesus is the best thing you can do for your spouse. The more you're like Jesus, the better your marriage will be. And that change starts when you see that you need it and ask God to work it.

### 3. REMEMBER WHO YOUR SPOUSE IS

James tells us we're selfish sinners who are in love with the world, and the only reason we're still in this thing with God is because he is incredibly gracious.

If your husband or wife is a Christian, that is true of them, too. One elder I know gives this advice to married guys (although the principle works both ways):

> *"Every day when you wake up, look at your wife and say to yourself, 'She is a saved sinner. She's not going to be perfect today. But that has not stopped God saving her, and that must not stop me loving her.'"*

No marriage is perfect, however much they might look that way on a Sunday in church. Every marriage has regrets and heartaches and sin that you don't see from the outside. So don't think that your marriage isn't working, or isn't worth it, because you're fighting sin or things have gone wrong. God can still be gracious. Yes, you're sinners—but in Christ, you're saved.

### 4. BE REALISTICALLY POSITIVE ABOUT SEX

The Bible is unapologetically positive about sex. It's the God-given means which cements husband and wife as "one flesh"—spiritually, emotionally and physically. (Or, to use the words of a considerably less obscure British band from a few decades ago, it's how "two become one").

Tim Chester describes it this way:

> "*Good sex is not about quality of technique, but about quality of relationship. Sex is not a "thing" that you do. It's inextricably embedded in a relationship. Its purpose is to celebrate and cement that relationship.*"
> *(Gospel Centred Marriage, page 84)*

But why does something so good turn into an area of so much struggle for so many couples? One friend put it like this:

> "*When I got married, I discovered that I'd absorbed more of our culture's view on sex than I'd realised. Culture says that sex is always and immediately smooth, slick and pleasurable. But it's not. And then you're left with this question of 'How am I meant to be loving in this situation that's actually kind of awkward and uncomfortable? How do you handle these mismatched levels of enjoyment?' It's definitely improved, but sex is still hard work. It doesn't just happen either—you sort of have to schedule it in. And if it's been a stressful day at work and everything else then... Well, yeah, it's OK.*"

She's not been married long, but I think she's asking the right question: "How am I meant to be loving in this situation?"

When it comes to sex, grace and humility look like serving your husband or wife, even when you don't really feel like it. They look like being able to take pleasure in giving pleasure. They look like being humble enough to recognise that it's OK if you turn out not to be a 21st-century Casanova. And they look like being humble enough to talk openly about sex, and ask what you could do to make it a better experience for your spouse.

## 5. PRAY

God "shows favour to the humble", and one of the ways we express humility is by praying. A humble spouse comes before God on their knees and admits that they don't have what it takes to be the husband or wife that they should be, or to make their marriage the picture of Christ and his church that it ought to be.

So pray for yourself, and pray for your spouse. It's almost impossible to do this too much. One friend put it like this: "If you're cross, pray for her. If you've had a lovely day together, pray for her. If she's struggling, don't just try to fix it; pray for her." The wonderful promise of James 4 v 6 is that God shows favour to those who admit that they need it.

## 6. JUST ENJOY IT

Am I allowed to say that it's possible to take marriage just a bit too seriously? Some people seem to be so focused on getting marriage "right" that they forget to appreciate it for what it is—a great gift from a gracious Father.

One way that we show gratitude for a gift is simply by enjoying it. So just have fun! Laugh with one another, be silly together, go exploring. All these little moments of love and intimacy are a picture of Christ and the church. Savour the everyday moments when you're just hanging out: the joy you get from simply being around one another. Take delight in 101 daily graces—and thank God for them.

## THE TWILIGHT WORLD OF DATING

Marriage is hard at times (and in some cases, for much of the time). But marriage is still great. It's good to be married. And that means it's good to seek to get married too. After all, "He who finds a wife finds a good thing" (Proverbs 18 v 22, ESV—and, of course, vice versa!)

Yet marriages don't just materialise out of nowhere. First you have to navigate the mysterious twilight zone in between... or as it's often known, dating. For some, it's a straightforward journey from A to B; for others, it's a circular mishmash of confused emotions and false starts. Either way, there's no map included.

But that twilight zone must only ever be a means to an end. In our 21st-century Western Christian culture, it's the way that two people work out whether or not they should get married. How long that takes depends on the individuals involved; but dating relationships should only go on for as long as it takes to reach clarity on that crucial question (with as much certainty as is humanly possible—which, for some of us, is never as much as we'd like). After that, it's time to put a ring on it or part ways. Both of those outcomes can be deemed a success if the relationship achieved what it was meant to—clarity.

This makes the dating stakes very high. Who we marry—or who we don't marry—is one of the biggest decisions we'll make. It's likely that we will literally be living with the consequences for the next 50 years. That's a slightly terrifying prospect! How do we go about getting this right?

Let's take those same verses from James 4 and apply them to Christian dating in the age of Tinder.

## 1. KNOW WHAT YOU'RE LOOKING FOR
This first point should go without saying: don't get in bed with the world. Not metaphorically, and not literally either.

James sounds pretty stark when he says that a person who isn't a Christian is "an enemy of God" (James 4 v 4)—including the fit ones. That means the non-Christians we know need our love and compassion. It's right to commit to being their friend and seeking to share the gospel with them.

But marriage is something far more intimate. Why would you throw your life's lot in with someone who is at war with the One you love most? Don't set yourself up for a choice between personal heartbreak and spiritual compromise. These relationships don't usually come out of nowhere either—if exchanging funny WhatsApp messages or having one-on-one drinks after work is feeding your feelings, then stop.

When it comes to marriage, you need to be married to someone who loves Jesus, or to no one. But that second option is in no way second best. Singleness is not a problem that needs fixing. (I just spent a whole chapter trying to convince you of that.)

"OK, OK, enough with the rant already," you might be thinking. "I'll only go out with a Christian. But the problem is... which Christian? Should I go out with *this* Christian?" You hear some people say things like, "If they're not married, not related and not an unbeliever, then go for it!" Which is fine, but like... do you need to fancy them too? Or feel some kind of attraction? And what does that even mean? What am I meant to feel, and when?

One person I know put it this way:

> *"If you're going to marry someone, then I think you've got to be excited about the prospect of living for Christ as a married couple and helping each other become more like him. And part of living for Christ as a married couple (although it is only part) is physical intimacy."*

That sounds like wisdom, I think—and it means two things.

First, that when we're thinking about marriage, the best question to ask is not simply, "Is this person a Christian?" but "Is this someone who can help me live for Christ and who I can help live for Christ themselves?" As you date someone, it's worth regularly, and honestly, returning to that question.

Second, it means that before getting married there does need to be some attraction towards physical intimacy. But we're all wired differently, and for some people that kind of attraction can sometimes only be fostered with time. Hence the dating.

All this is particularly important to remember in the world of online dating, where how much we really know about a person is virtually zero. If you meet someone at church, you can be fairly confident that you'll be on the same page theologically. Or if you have mutual friends, you can trust their judgement of this person's character. But online dating widens the pool considerably. This means that, if we're going down the online route, we probably need to be more careful and more deliberate in working out whether this is someone with whom we can be excited about living for Christ as a married couple.

## 2. BE HUMBLE—TAKE A RISK
If "God opposes the proud but shows favour to the humble", what does that mean when it comes to dating?

Sometimes pride looks like never being prepared to take a risk to ask someone out or pursue a relationship, because you can't bear the thought of being rejected or of things going wrong. Pride also looks like never being prepared to take a chance on someone who's godly but a little bit different, because you care too much about what other people think. Pride expects a potential date to score 10/10 on every category (or, at a push, an 8), because that's what you deserve.

More than anything, pride hates anything awkward, because awkward feels weak and looks bad. And let's face it: dating can be incredibly awkward. One recently married friend told me:

> *"When we think back to the early stages of our dating, we laugh about how awkward it was. We used to go for these walks round the park on a Sunday afternoon to talk things over... There were so many awkward moments. But I'm so glad we persevered and pushed through it."*

Humility, on the other hand, isn't afraid of looking or feeling weak. Humility grows when we know that we have a big God who is in control of our lives, and when it's his love and acceptance that matter most to us. Which means that we can take a risk, knowing that if things don't work out, that will be OK. Humility doesn't flirt just to feed your ego, or string someone along because you can't make your mind up. Instead, humility means you're honest and open about where things are going and how fast, because you're not trying to look good.

### 3. BE HUMBLE—GET ADVICE

If you don't think you need anyone else to hold you accountable, you're probably seriously overestimating your own godliness.

If a Christian friend raises a question over the way you're conducting yourself with a member of the opposite sex, be humble enough to seriously consider their words. Is there truth—even an element of truth—to what they are saying?

One area where we're offered a lot of advice is on "how far is too far". I'm not going to add any more—but I am going to say that we need to listen to those who are older and wiser than us, even if it doesn't seem to make much sense. A humble attitude says, "I might not like what you're saying or agree with it; but I'm prepared to accept that you might know something that I don't."

Humility doesn't just accept advice—it seeks it out. If you're dating someone and you're trying to work out whether to marry them, then at some point it's probably wise to seek the advice of your parents (and, perhaps, some "spiritual parents" in your own church). That's not a conversation that starts with, "Mum, Dad, isn't he great?" It goes more like, "Mum, Dad, what do you really think? I want you to be honest and I'm ready to listen."

## 4. EMBRACE GRACE
Sometimes, in the twilight world of dating, Christians make mistakes—either in maintaining sexual purity or in caring for another's heart. It's never justifiable. But it is always forgivable. If we make a mess of it, God "gives us more grace" (v 6). Nothing you've done puts you beyond the reaches of his forgiveness. Making a mistake doesn't mean that you need to break up necessarily, but it does mean you need to get on a better track. If you're not really committed to each other's holiness, you're not really committed to each other at all.

One way or another, we'll need grace as a relationship continues. And if it does not continue, then we will need grace too—grace to remember that that person is our brother or sister before they're our ex. That isn't always easy, but it is always possible—and it is always preferable to holding on to hurts.

## 5. PRAY
If you're not married and you want to be married, pray about it. After all, James says, "You do not have because you do not ask God" (v 2). That sort of logic makes my theological senses twitch—yet it's there in Scripture. There's a place for simply asking God to provide you with a godly husband or wife. He's a generous Father.

"MY MARRIAGE ADVICE: REMEMBER THERE'S MORE THAN ONE WAY TO STACK A DISHWASHER."

#ISTHISIT

But remember that it's possible that:

> *... when you ask, you do not receive, because you ask with wrong motives, that you may spend what you get on your pleasures. (v 3)*

Don't just pray for marriage—pray about your motives. Ask God to show you where your thinking is falling into fear, or pride, or selfishness, and how that is playing out in the way you treat your brothers or sisters or think about your future. Pray that you would desire marriage and date others for the right reasons.

## 6. JUST ENJOY IT

Like marriage, it is possible to take dating a bit too seriously. Some people seem to place the same significance on asking a girl to go for coffee as they do on asking her for her hand in marriage. That means no one goes on any dates because they're never that sure; and no one's ever that sure because they never go on any dates.

Sometimes, we just need to lighten up. After all, there's joy to be had just in getting to know someone. If every time you see someone you're aiming to love them like Jesus would and show them something of him, you really can't go too far wrong.

# OF GRACE AND DISHWASHERS

> *But he gives us more grace. That is why Scripture says: "God opposes the proud but shows favour to the humble".*

It's a great verse—two sentences that contain a relationship's-worth of help and advice. Still, on balance, next time I'm asked to give a tip to a couple-to-be, I think I'll stick with:

*Remember there's more than one way to stack a dishwasher.*

# 10. GETTING OLD
## I THINK I'M ACTUALLY GOING TO DIE ONE DAY

For me, it's grey hair. I look for it, hide it, pluck it, and give up on it. One day soon I'll have to start dyeing it (but I'm putting that off as long as possible because, you know... *effort*). All this makes me sad because I kinda like my hair. It's long and brown and shiny and curly... but, increasingly, grey.

That's what makes me feel old. And I hate it.

What is it for you?

Maybe it's the fact that you've lost both the desire and the ability to stay up past midnight very often. Or the realisation that pop music's really not what it used to be. Or your baffled confusion at the "youth speak" today's teenagers converse in.

Perhaps it's something to do with your body. There comes a "tipping point" where we stop getting taller and stronger with every birthday as we get older. Now we're just... getting older. Maybe it's a receding hairline that's getting harder and harder to cover up. Or a twinge of pain in your lower back. Or the prescription for your glasses that's leaping up at a greater rate than your age. Or maybe all this sounds incredibly trivial, because you're facing up to serious health problems in your 20s.

When we feel old, most of us deal with it using one of the following options:

1. Wail "I'm sooooo old" with a sense of despair.

2. Shut up about it, try to forget about it, and hope that no one will notice whatever tell-tale sign you're trying to ignore (or at least, that if they do notice it, they won't mention it).

3. Redouble your efforts on your health and fitness routines.

4. Console yourself with a tub of ice cream, a few beers, and/or the fact that at least you're not as old as someone else.

(OK, there is one more—we'll get to that later on.)

Whether or not you have a fraught relationship with aging, it's fair to say that our culture definitely does. Most people are desperate to deny it or delay it, and there's a £500-billion ($675-billion) beauty industry out there to prove it. Our TV screens and newspaper gossip columns are filled with people who are young and beautiful. I guess that no one wants to be reminded of the reality that most of us are neither of those things, and that none of us are both of those things for very long.

None of this is very constructive—and you know it. Buzzfeed knows it too. Here's some advice in an article titled "15 Things You Need To Stop Doing During Your Quarter-Life Crisis":

> "STOP *thinking about the fact that you are inching closer to death, osteoporosis, and dying alone. Repeatedly saying 'I'm so old' will not make you feel better. Also, it makes people who are actually older than you want to slap you in the face.*"

In one sense, Buzzfeed is right to remind us that we're not that old really, and that we'd be wise to put our (relatively) youthful energy to good use. But in another sense, Buzzfeed's advice is not much use at all. What person has ever stopped thinking about something by trying to stop thinking about it? Besides which, if something is inevitably going to happen, then it probably *is* worth thinking about.

So that's what we're going to do—because it's only by confronting the truth that we can replace our sense of despair with a sense of perspective.

When we look in the mirror and get that sinking feeling, we need someone to shake us by the metaphorical shoulders and tell us what we need to hear. And that someone doing the shaking needs to be you.

Next time you feel old, here are three things to tell yourself.

## 1. I'M NOT AGEING, I'M DYING (I KNOW THIS DOESN'T MAKE YOU WANT TO READ ON. IT GETS MORE CHEERFUL. I PROMISE.)

That statement is not a very upbeat place to start a pep-talk. It's blunt. It's uncomfortable. You may even be slightly offended at seeing the fact of your own mortality laid out like that on the page. If you are, that's fair enough—here's why.

Ageing reminds us that time is running out. The reality is that I don't have my whole life ahead of me—at the very best, 20% of it is behind me (and who knows, perhaps 99% of it is). When I see a grey hair, I see a clock whose hands are turning at an alarming speed. It reminds me that there are things I want to do, and places I want to go, that I'll probably never get round to.

Some of these desires for our lives are good, God-given ones— such as the desire to see people we love come to faith, or to get married and have a family. The biological clock is real, and for many people—women especially—it starts ticking loudly in our 20s. My friend Lauren said her Quarter-Life Crisis was marked by a profound sense of loss, as she grieved things she has never had and maybe never will.

I suspect that most of us fear old age itself, too. It certainly looks like a tough gig: the ill-health, the weariness, the indignity, the loneliness. It's easy to start thinking that each grey hair I see in the mirror brings me closer to what I'll look like when I'm old and alone in a care home... and when I'm dead in a coffin.

Ageing is a symptom of the terminal condition we're all suffering from: mortality. We're not just ageing; we're dying. And death is horrible. That's how Moses (almost) puts it in Psalm 90:

> *Lord, you have been our dwelling-place*
> *throughout all generations.*
> *Before the mountains were born*
> *or you brought forth the whole world,*
> *from everlasting to everlasting you are God.*
> *You turn people back to dust,*
> *saying, "Return to dust, you mortals."*
> *A thousand years in your sight*
> *are like a day that has just gone by,*
> *or like a watch in the night.*
> *Yet you sweep people away in the sleep of death—*
> *they are like the new grass of the morning:*
> *In the morning it springs up new,*
> *but by evening it is dry and withered. (v 1-6)*

We're right to feel that life is short, because it is. Whereas God is from "everlasting to everlasting" (v 2), we're not. Moses reminds us that our whole lifetime—including all our achievements and victories—is like a day in God's millennium. We're like grass:

there are lots of us, our existence is short-lived, and there's really nothing much that we can do about it. We're powerless blades of grass, quivering in front of a lawnmower called Time.

Some of us have experienced this reality in a painfully personal way. "I think the watershed moment for me in my 20s was when my friend's dad died," Matt told me. "It was awful. I realised there was nothing I could do to make it less painful; nothing I could do to make it less sad. I was powerless." Death is a problem we cannot solve—either for others or ourselves:

*We finish our years with a moan.*
*Our days may come to seventy years,*
  *or eighty, if our strength endures;*
*yet the best of them are but trouble and sorrow,*
  *for they quickly pass, and we fly away. (v 9b-10)*

So far, so miserable. But don't miss *why* this is the case.

*We are consumed by your anger*
  *and terrified by your indignation.*
*You have set our iniquities before you,*
  *our secret sins in the light of your presence.*
*All our days pass away under your wrath;*
  *we finish our years with a moan.*
*Our days may come to seventy years,*
  *or eighty, if our strength endures;*
*yet the best of them are but trouble and sorrow,*
  *for they quickly pass, and we fly away.*
*If only we knew the power of your anger!*
  *Your wrath is as great as the fear that is your due. (v 7-9)*

Our troubles and sorrows show us that all is not well between the world and its Creator—and our own death is the final expression of God's wrath: his right, justified anger at our sin.

If I think of God as making his judgment of me based only on my external, public behaviour that other people can see, then it becomes tempting to think that God is unfair to be quite so angry (although there are people who know me who'd beg to differ). But the terrifying reality is that God sees and exposes even the "secret sins"—there's nothing I think truly in private, and there's nothing I do truly alone.

Imagine all those things about you that you're relieved no one else knows. The stuff you've done that you're glad the guys at work and your friends at church have no idea about. The things you've thought that you'd hate anyone to find out about. And behind all that, there's the attitude—the attitude that tells God that you don't want him to be the boss of you, and that you'd be better off running your life without him. God sees all of it, and he's angry.

Ageing is a symptom of dying, and dying is a symptom of rejecting the One who gives life.

If the fact of your mortality makes you sad, then good—it ought to. But not because it shows you're running out of time to do all that you want to do. In fact, quite the opposite. Mortality is sad because it shows that you—along with everyone else—have been doing precisely what you want to do all along. And now you're facing death as a result. It is desperately, desperately sad.

The right response to ageing is not to deny it or to try to delay it, but to own it. That's what Moses does:

> *Teach us to number our days,*
>   *that we may gain a heart of wisdom. (v 12)*

He's saying, *If we truly understood that we're dying, and that we deserve to die, then we'd start approaching life with the right attitude.*

So follow Moses' advice. Let the fact that you're ageing remind you of *why* you are ageing—let each grey hair or lost hair teach you to "number [your] days". Let it increase your fear of God and your horror at sin. Remember that the longer you live, and the more lines on your face you accumulate, the more "secret sins" you will have to repent of; let the glimpses you get of the ageing process prompt you to confess to God the reason behind it. Don't lament your age without looking inwards to lament your sin, and looking outwards to lament all the broken consequences of a world in rebellion.

Ageing should make us sad—because sin is horrible. When you feel old, tell yourself, *I'm not just ageing; I'm dying, because the world is under God's wrath.*

## 2. I'M DYING, BUT I'M LIVING

But that shouldn't be the only thing you tell yourself. In fact, if you flick on just a page in your Bible to Psalm 92, you'll find a radically different picture of ageing:

> *The righteous will flourish like a palm tree,*
> *    they will grow like a cedar of Lebanon;*
> *planted in the house of the LORD,*
> *    they will flourish in the courts of our God.*
> *They will still bear fruit in old age,*
> *    they will stay fresh and green,*
> *proclaiming, "The LORD is upright;*
> *    he is my Rock, and there is no wickedness in him."*
>
> *(Psalm 92 v 12-15)*

Whereas Moses compared us to withering grass, this writer says that it's possible to be a flourishing tree. I associate "palm trees" with a dream retirement cruise around the Caribbean. But the psalmist is probably imagining these trees' height and strength—when you think palm tree, the writer wants you to think regal, dignified, steady, beautiful. It's possible to be all of those things as we age.

So what it is that makes the difference between dying grass and living trees? These trees are drawing their nutrients from roots "planted in the house of the LORD" (v 13). In the Old Testament, this meant the temple: the place that was filled with God's presence and that was the focal point of the Israelites' relationship with their God.

Believers today don't have a physical temple, but it's still in living in God's presence that we flourish. This goes much deeper than an age-defying face cream. We flourish as we dwell in him and he dwells in us by his Spirit—as we draw his spiritual sap up through our roots and let it fill our bloodstream and transform our hearts. As Jesus put it:

*I am the vine; you are the branches. If you remain in me and I in you, you will bear much fruit; apart from me you can do nothing. (John 15 v 5)*

As we do that, we "bear fruit" (Psalm 92 v 14). Fruit like love, joy, peace, patience, kindness, goodness, faithfulness, gentleness and self-control. There's no age limit on producing this fruit—in fact, if we're rooted properly in Christ, then the yield is only going to increase over time.

Think of it this way: the longer you live, the more opportunities you'll have to experience that God is a "Rock"—that he is "upright" and wholly good (v 15). I don't know what will happen to you in the next few decades; but I do know that you will be able view whatever happens as proof that God is faithful. And the more clearly you see that, the more confidently you can proclaim that truth to others.

# FIND YOUR ENID

One of the reasons that we fear growing old is because our Western culture tells us every day, in a hundred different ways, that youth is better. The Bible disagrees. "Grey hair is a crown of splendour; it is attained in the way of righteousness" (Proverbs 16 v 31). Being an older Christian means (or should mean) that you're a wiser Christian, with more experience of life's trials and triumphs, and so better able to encourage and advise younger Christians (Titus 2 v 3-5). In the church it really is meant to be a case of "age before beauty"—which means that those of us who are younger can, and should, look at our elders not with pity or fear but respect and love.

I really hope that you know an older person who is like the trees in Psalm 92. I hope there's someone who's a stage of life or two (or six) ahead of you, who, when you're around them, makes you think, "Wow, I really want to be like them when I'm older, because they're really like Jesus".

For me, she's called Enid. Enid is 91, and is part of the church that I grew up in. She seemed kind of old when I sang in the church choir with her as a kid. Now she seems even older— her steps are small and slow, her back is all bent over, and the joints in her hands are swollen. But whenever I'm visiting my parents' church, and I kneel down by her chair to say hello, and take those gnarled, shaking hands in mine, I can see that on the inside Enid is a flourishing cedar tree—tall, strong and fruitful. She's always thrilled to see me, and is interested in how I'm doing. She speaks about life with an infectious sense of joy. And although Enid's ageing body frustrates her, she's so looking forward to the day when she'll meet Jesus in heaven and be free of all pain.

When I'm older, I really want to be like Enid.

When we think of ageing as an opportunity to grow, we can look forward to it rather than simply dreading it. Think back and look at how far God has brought you already—the ways that he's worked in you to change you for the better, and worked through you for the good of others—and be excited that there's so much more of that to come. If that's what God can do with you in a couple of years or a couple of decades, can you imagine what he is able to do with you in the next 60 years?

So each time you look in the mirror and are tempted to despair at what you see, let it prompt you to pray. Pray that your increasing years will be matched by increasing wisdom. Ask God to help you to look at, look after, and long to be like the godly older believers you know. Give thanks that "though outwardly we are wasting away, yet inwardly we are being renewed day by day" (2 Corinthians 4 v 16). Then ask God to keep changing you, so that one day you will be "fresh and green" even if you are old and grey (Psalm 92 v 14).

## 3. I'M LIVING, THEN I'M RISING

Our souls can be evergreen—and there's hope for our ageing bodies too. There's hope for backs that ache and pains that stay and dreams that fade with the passing of time. That hope lies in a one-word promise: resurrection.

The first-century Greek city of Corinth was a youthful, cosmopolitan place. Its citizens prized the physical pleasures of sex and beauty. But in his letter for the Christians there, the apostle Paul describes their bodies—from the gym nuts to the beauty queens—as mere seeds: small, shrivelled, unimpressive... and dead. And that's great—because it's once you see your body as a seed that you're able to get excited about what will happen when you're buried in the ground:

> *The body that is sown is perishable, it is raised imperishable;*
> *it is sown in dishonour, it is raised in glory; it is sown in*
> *weakness, it is raised in power; it is sown a natural body, it*
> *is raised a spiritual body. (1 Corinthians 15 v 42-44)*

One day in the future—on a day that God has already marked in his calendar—we will each receive a new body that is imperishable, glorious, strong, and in some way "spiritual". But it'll be physical too, and we'll be raised to live on a physical new earth—we're not going to spend eternity floating around as ghosts in white sheets. These new bodies will be as real as our "natural" bodies are now—but they'll be turbo-charged with life and health and strength.

Our bodies now fail us and frustrate us; our new bodies won't. Time in these bodies is running out fast; time in our new bodies will last for ever. On resurrection day, it won't matter that we never ticked Bali off the bucket list while we were in our natural body. It won't matter that we never had the family we wanted to. The physical sensations of life in our new bodies will eclipse any experience we have, or miss out on having, here.

And whereas the ageing process is gradual—one fine line on the face at a time—its reversal will happen in the blink of an eye:

> *Listen, I tell you a mystery: we will not all sleep, but we*
> *will all be changed—in a flash, in the twinkling of an eye,*
> *at the last trumpet. For the trumpet will sound, the dead*
> *will be raised imperishable, and we will be changed. For*
> *the perishable must clothe itself with the imperishable,*
> *and the mortal with immortality. When the perishable has*
> *been clothed with the imperishable, and the mortal with*
> *immortality, then the saying that is written will come true:*
> *"Death has been swallowed up in victory." (v 51-54)*

"WHEN YOU LOOK IN THE MIRROR, LOOK PAST THE DAY WHEN YOUR HAIR WILL BE GREY TO THE DAY WHEN IT WILL BE GOLDEN."

#ISTHISIT

So when you look in the mirror, look past the day when your hair will be grey to the day when it will be golden.

I find this so hard—but perhaps that's because grey hairs are pretty much the worst I have to contend with right now. It's enough to provoke my vanity, but rarely is it enough to make me long for the prospect of my resurrection body. The problem is that the more comfortable I am now, the more I want to hold on to this moment in time. Yet I can think of a Christian I know in her early thirties who has suffered much, and lost a great deal, including many of her dreams—but is so looking forward to the new creation as a result. She speaks about it with a natural enthusiasm that I find hard to muster. She's...

> "... *excitedly [longing] for the day when we can each look back and, informed not by faith but by sight, say, 'Paul was right! Nothing—no pleasure or pain in that momentary time I had before I arrived here—can compare to being at home with my Saviour, living in the fullness of being all that God created me to be, and basking in his eternal presence and glory.'"* (Sarah Walton, Hope When It Hurts, page 178)

Every snatch of frustration with our bodies now—small though those frustrations are in our 20s for most (although not all) of us—is an opportunity to fix our eyes on the new bodies we're heading towards. Start ageing with grace now, and you've got more chance of ageing gracefully in the years ahead; after all, this is one quarter-life issue that's not going to go away.

But more than rejoicing at the prospect of a new body, rejoice in the One who makes this possible. That's where Paul ends up:

> *The sting of death is sin, and the power of sin is the law. But thanks be to God! He gives us the victory through our Lord Jesus Christ. (v 56-57)*

However hard we try, we're always losing the fight against age—but Christ has won the victory against sin. The moment of death will have no sting, and our existence beyond death will have no pain or regret because on the cross Christ has already taken the sting of God's wrath and the experience of hell for us. Instead we can enjoy perfect joy in perfect bodies in a perfect world with our perfect Saviour, for ever. "Thanks be to God!"

And until that day, you're called to "give yourselves fully to the work of the Lord, because you know that your labour in the Lord is not in vain" (v 58). Because he's a Saviour who has given you eternal life, he's worth living for wholeheartedly in this life, with every day you have left.

## LOOK IN THE MIRROR

So when you look in the mirror, or at the number of candles on your birthday cake, and resent what you see, here's what to tell yourself. If it helps, write it out and stick it up somewhere where you'll see it. In fact, get up now, look at yourself in the mirror, and tell yourself this:

"I'm dying"—so repent, confessing the sin that makes death inevitable.

"I'm living"—so request, asking God to make you more spiritually fruitful the older you get.

"I'm rising"—so rejoice, giving thanks to Christ for dying and rising to guarantee your resurrection body.

And then, once you've reminded yourself of all that, it's time to stop looking in the mirror and start doing something with your day.

# 11. MEANINGLESS

## WHAT'S THE POINT?

Congratulations. If you're reading this chapter, it's probably because you have realised in just a couple of decades
what many people take much longer to figure out: life is
meaningless.

If you think that's a melodramatic start to a chapter, you
should try the Old Testament book of Ecclesiastes. The
writer, who calls himself "the Teacher", is the "son of David,
king of Jerusalem" (Ecclesiastes 1 v 1)—most likely Solomon,
who at the peak of his rule was the wisest man who ever lived
(bar one). This is equivalent to saying, *Note to reader: this is a
guy with something worthwhile to say.*

And what's the first thing he says?

> *Meaningless! Meaningless! ... Utterly meaningless!*
> *Everything is meaningless! (v 2)*

This is not the kind of verse you'd share on Instagram with a
brush-script font over some classy background photography.

So what is it that makes life so utterly pointless? The Teacher
starts by reflecting on the endless cycles of nature. It's like he's
watching a nature documentary on loop:

*Generations come and generations go,*
  *but the earth remains for ever.*
*The sun rises and the sun sets,*
  *and hurries back to where it rises.*
*The wind blows to the south*
  *and turns to the north;*
*round and round it goes,*
  *ever returning on its course.*
*All streams flow into the sea,*
  *yet the sea is never full.*
*To the place streams come from,*
  *there they return again. (v 4-7)*

Now, we don't know how old the Teacher was when he wrote this—but if he had ever had to commute, we can guess that he'd have had this existential crisis in his 20s. Most of us aren't long out of education before we know what it's like to lose heart in the cycle of the daily grind: eat, sleep, work, repeat.

And all this is part of a larger "life cycle": school, college, maybe university... job, marriage, house, kids. And then those kids grow up and go to school, college, maybe university... and so it continues (and, eventually, ends).

Our existence when we were teenagers and students felt like a straight line: life was broken up into manageable, year-by-year chunks, all purposefully working towards the time when we'd be "out there" in the big wide world. Then we get "out there", and it all turns a bit circular. And perhaps, like the Teacher, you find yourself wondering... *why?*

## DISTRACTION TACTICS

Most of us don't ask ourselves the uncomfortable "Why?" question very often, because humans are experts at keeping themselves busy: "The eye never has enough of seeing, nor the ear its fill of hearing" (v 8). Our media-soaked age gives us a constant supply of content to fill our hungry eyes and ears. We're always looking to entertain ourselves as we mindlessly click on to the next article on the news app, or the next song on our playlist, or the next level on the game on our phone. Even if we're not entertained, at least we're distracted from the pitiable meaninglessness of the whole charade.

The Teacher gives these distraction tactics a go too. He embarks on a search for meaning, and in the process tries almost all of our culture's 20-or-30-something aspirations:

- Fun times with friends. "Laughter ... is madness. And what does pleasure accomplish?" (2 v 2).

- Big nights out with the guys. "I tried cheering myself with wine, and embracing folly" (v 3).

- Countless Tinder hook-ups. "I acquired ... a harem as well—the delights of a man's heart" (v 8).

- Buying his "forever home". "I undertook great projects: I built houses for myself and planted vineyards" (v 4).

- Decorating his forever home with quirky artwork from his backpacking trip around South-east Asia. "I amassed ... the treasure of kings and provinces" (v 8).

- Climbing the career ladder. "I also owned more herds and flocks than anyone in Jerusalem before me" (v 7).

- Negotiating a pay rise. "I amassed silver and gold for myself" (v 8).

- Finding fame in his field. "I became greater by far than anyone in Jerusalem before me" (v 9).

If I had the Teacher as a friend on Facebook, I'd probably hide his irritating photographs and smug status updates from my newsfeed. He certainly seems to enjoy his work-hard-play-hard lifestyle for a while:

> *I denied myself nothing my eyes desired;*
>   *I refused my heart no pleasure.*
> *My heart took delight in all my labour. (v 10)*

But in the end, nothing can distract him enough. The truth gapes open like a void at his feet. In the very next verse, all of his achievements get the same damning verdict:

> *Yet when I surveyed all that my hands had done*
>   *and what I had toiled to achieve,*
> *everything was meaningless, a chasing after the wind;*
>   *nothing was gained under the sun. (v 11)*

Maybe you know this feeling. Maybe you've tried more things on that list than you'd want to admit to your pastor, or your gran—and none of it really satisfied. What was the point? Or maybe you're in a wholesome but steady routine of church and work and time with friends and family. You're working hard, meeting your goals, enjoying your youth, and generally having a nice time. But sometimes—when you're groping for your alarm in the morning, or looking at the other commuters crowded onto the train, or staring at the sky at night—a quiet voice inside of you asks that same question: "What's the point?"

It's a very unpleasant sensation, and the Teacher knows it. "So I hated life," he concludes: "My heart began to despair" (v 17, 20).

## I WANNA LEAVE MY FOOTPRINTS

So what's the cause of this existential despair? What is it that makes life meaningless? The Teacher tells us:

*I hated all the things I had toiled for under the sun, because I must leave them to the one who comes after me. (v 18)*

Let me put it even more bluntly than that: death makes life meaningless. Whatever we achieve in the next 50 or 60 years, we'll all meet the same fate. The size of our salary, the state of our bucket list, even how happy our existence has been—it will all mean nothing once we're dead.

The impending reality of death colours everything in the meantime, and snatches our joy if we think about it long enough. If we look for meaning in trying to build a legacy to leave behind, the Teacher says that we're kidding ourselves. "No one remembers the former generations, and even those yet to come will not be remembered by those who follow them" (1 v 11).

If we look for meaning in trying to do something innovative to improve the state of humanity, the Teacher says that we're wasting our time too: "What has been will be again, what has been done will be done again; there is nothing new under the sun" (v 9).

If we look for meaning in trying to accomplish something durable—looking for a life-size sense of achievement around the other side of that huge work project or the next life milestone—we'll be disappointed. "What is crooked cannot be straightened; what is lacking cannot be counted" (v 15). Most of us get a sense of this in our jobs. If you're a nurse, there will always be more sick people to care for. If you're a waiter, there will always be more tables to clear. If you're a computer programmer, there will always be more bugs to fix. The good that we do is eventually unravelled—people age, mess gets made, systems break—and we have to do it again. These are all like mini-deaths in a world under a terminal diagnosis.

So death makes life meaningless—or, in the words of the Teacher, "a chasing after the wind"—because there's nothing we can hold on to. Death unravels all our hard work. Even the things that seem to mean the most—those relationships we treasure—will ultimately be undone by death.

Life is meaningless.

And yet... all of us find this so hard to accept. We long for our lives to mean something. To paraphrase Beyoncé, I want to do something or leave something that means I leave my footprints on the sands of time—that proves that I was here, and that my time on Planet Earth made a difference somehow. There's something deep within us that refuses to settle for the notion that our existence is insignificant. You could say that that "something"—that longing for a bigger reality—is what makes us human. But in order to find the meaning we crave, we need to find a solution to the problem of the grave.

And the good news is, there is someone who can give us that.

## MAKE LIFE MEANINGFUL
Fast-forward about 1,000 years in Bible history to another teacher—Jesus of Nazareth:

> *Whoever wants to be my disciple must deny themselves and take up their cross and follow me. For whoever wants to save their life will lose it, but whoever loses their life for me will find it. What good will it be for someone to gain the whole world, yet forfeit their soul? Or what can anyone give in exchange for their soul? (Matthew 16 v 24-26)*

Whereas the Teacher in Ecclesiastes despaired in the face of death, Jesus is far more than a teacher—he is a Saviour, who calls us to follow him through death.

"THERE'S SOMETHING DEEP WITHIN US THAT REFUSES TO SETTLE FOR THE NOTION THAT OUR EXISTENCE IS INSIGNIFICANT."

#ISTHISIT

So where is Jesus heading, exactly? Immediately before these words of Jesus, Matthew describes the watershed moment when Peter rightly identifies Jesus as "the Messiah"—a Hebrew word to describe God's universal, all-powerful rescuing King. But Peter misunderstands how this rescue will be brought about:

> *[Jesus began to explain that he] must go to Jerusalem and suffer many things at the hands of the elders, the chief priests and the teachers of the law, and that he must be killed and on the third day be raised to life. (v 21)*

Because Jesus is walking towards his own death and resurrection, he's able to offer life to those who follow him.

What he has in mind when he talks about "finding life" in verse 25 is, of course, eternal life. Eternal life is like a spiritual heart which starts beating when we begin to follow Jesus, and which continues beating for ever, even when the pump in our chests stops. It's a life that's not rendered meaningless by death, because death is just a comma, not a full stop—death catapults us into a dazzling reality of purpose and beauty and joy, unaffected by the mini-deaths and frustrations which hamper our existence now. It's a life lived in the personal presence of the Lord of everything—where the King who loved us enough to take up his cross meets us face to face.

To enjoy the life that Jesus gives, we have to stop trying to hold on to and build life ourselves. That's what Jesus means when he says that "whoever wants to save their life will lose it", and "whoever loses their life for me will find it". Christians sometimes call this "dying to self".

So often, my longing for meaning is really a longing for *me* to mean something. I want me to be important. I want *my* life to be significant. So I cling to it, build it, protect it, desperately hoping that somehow it will reach the status of "worthwhile".

Yet Jesus says I need to lose my life. That means we have to stop trying to carve out a meaningful existence for ourselves by building our own reputation or amassing wealth—or even by doing good or bringing happiness to others. We have to repent of putting ourselves at the centre of our own universe and put Jesus there instead. At the end of the day, me-and-my-life doesn't need to mean anything—because Jesus means everything without me.

There's a reason that Jesus calls this shift in attitude "losing your life"—because it hurts. Sometimes when I remember that I am not, and will never be, the centre of the universe, it makes me genuinely sad.

Yet there's just no other option that makes sense. I might be in my 20s now, but soon I will be in my 80s, and then soon I will be dead. In the haunting logic of Jesus, "What good will it be for someone to gain the whole world, yet forfeit their soul?" If we try to hold on to life—seeking to make ourselves mean something by building a career, having a family, or writing Christian books—we will have gained much but lost the one thing that matters.

Although the cost is high, the rewards are massive. Lose your life like this, and Jesus guarantees that you will find it. Eternal life doesn't start when we die—if you're a follower of Jesus, you already have it. Life with him is abundant and overflowing and satisfying and, yes, meaningful, because it's free from the power of death. Because this life is eternal, it means that you can do stuff today which will endure for 200 years, or 200,000 years. Embrace Christ's topsy-turvy mindset, and you find the fulfilment you were looking for all along.

Death makes life meaningless. But dying-to-self makes life meaningful.

## WELL DONE

So how do we spend the next 50 or 60 years doing the stuff that matters?

A little later in Matthew's Gospel, in chapter 25, Jesus tells the parable of the bags of gold. You probably know the gist of it. A man is going on a journey, and while he's away, he entrusts his wealth to three servants. One servant gets five bags of gold, another gets three, and another gets one—crucially, the money is handed out to "each according to his ability" (v 15).

This detail is important to remember. Everyone is in a different God-given situation. We have different socio-economic backgrounds, different physical, mental and social strengths and weaknesses, different health circumstances, different opportunities, different spiritual gifts. It's God who hands out these resources, and he doesn't expect back from us more than he's resourced us for.

In the parable, the man who got five bags of gold "went at once and put his money to work and gained five bags more" (v 16). So did the second guy: "The one with two bags of gold gained two more" (v 17). And they both got the same response from their master on his return: "Well done, good and faithful servant! You have been faithful with a few things; I will put you in charge of many things. Come and share your master's happiness!" (v 21, 23).

The way that we die to self day by day is by recognising that every detail of our lives has been given to us by God, and is to be invested for his glory, not our own. The amount of "profit" we make doesn't matter so much. It's the servants' faithfulness—not their fruitfulness—that the master praises: "Well done, good and faithful servant! You have been faithful with a few things; I will put you in charge of many things."

This frees us from the tyranny of trying to build meaning out of how much we achieve. Our society likes to think it is a meritocracy—that anyone who wants to achieve can achieve. But the reality is that—along with a whole host of other factors—you're much more likely to "achieve" if you grew up in an affluent home than a poor one.

You might feel trapped by your circumstances. Maybe you're struggling to make ends meet. Other people have parents who can help them out, but you don't. Or maybe you're a carer for someone in your family, and you don't enjoy the freedom that many of your peers do. Or maybe something that happened to you years ago still clouds your physical or mental health today. If that's you, Jesus frees you from our culture's expectations that you've got to achieve something to mean something. Instead, he calls you to be faithful to him, however you can; to invest what he's given you—even if what he's given you doesn't feel like much—into his kingdom.

And if you do, you'll be met with the same response as someone else who seems to have all the gifts and all the opportunities. You'll receive the same ringing endorsement from your heavenly Father: "Well done!" If you're denying yourself and following Jesus, God is cheering you on with a hearty "Well done!" even if no one else is. And one day when you die, you'll be welcomed into your heavenly home with these words: "Come and share your master's happiness". Every faithful servant of Jesus is heading for an eternity of inexpressible joy, in relationship with him.

But the third servant in Jesus' story serves as a warning: "the man who had received one bag went off, dug a hole in the ground and hid his master's money" (v 18). We're not told what this third servant did with himself while the other servants were busy putting their master's money to work. Perhaps he went backpacking around Thailand. Maybe he completed some video games on his PS4. Or perhaps he lost a lot of weight and got into CrossFit. But when the master returns, and the servant gives him back the bag of gold, he's not happy: "You wicked, lazy servant! ... You should have put my money on deposit with the bankers, so that when I returned I would have received it back with interest" (v 26-27). The servant is wicked because he has robbed the master of what is rightfully his. He is lazy because he refused to work hard for the master. So he's not invited in to share in the master's happiness—he's thrown "outside, into the darkness, where there will be weeping and gnashing of teeth" (v 30).

This warns us against taking what God has given us and failing to do anything with it—against low expectations and low ambition. We mustn't conclude that everything is meaningless so we might as well do nothing with our lives. What we do now does mean something, because it means something *to God*.

Your time, capabilities, energy and money are all "gold" that has been graciously loaned to you by God. Don't settle for burying it. Invest it.

## IT LOOKS LIKE...
So what does that look like?

A lot of the time, it looks like setting out chairs and serving up coffee. It looks like making a meal for a new mum. It looks like ringing your grandad who lives on his own—and ringing someone else's grandad too. It looks like babysitting for a family so that a single parent can get out to a meeting. It looks like playing basketball with kids at a youth club. It looks like sitting next to someone you don't know on a Sunday and taking an interest in their life. It looks like telling your colleagues about Jesus. It looks like driving an older lady to the shops or to church. It looks like taking a risk to invite people round. It looks like photocopying and stapling and folding.

This is dying to self—and it hurts. It's biting your tongue when you'd rather criticise. It's opening your mouth when you'd rather stay quiet. It's opening up when you'd rather shut down. It's turning up when you'd rather stay home.

Let me tell you about my friend Myke. Myke is 28, has always lived with his mum, and doesn't have a girlfriend. He thought about moving abroad ("because that's what people seem to do") and even took an English-teaching qualification, but then bottled it. He works 30 hours a week at a school supporting a little boy with educational needs. He doesn't earn very much money. Worst of all, perhaps, he drives a Fiat.

By the world's estimation, he hasn't done much with the first decade of his adult life. But I'm pretty sure that won't be Jesus' verdict.

Myke heads up the group for 5-7-year-olds at our church. His job means that he's free at 4:30 p.m. on a Wednesday evening to lead the midweek club for 20 or so ordinary little kids from the neighbourhood. Many of them come from non-church homes—and for one hour a week, they get to hear about Jesus. And all because Myke is faithfully investing his gold. He writes lessons and teaches memory verses. He encourages the little ones to sit still so that they can listen. He heads up the team and gathers the leaders for a monthly prayer meeting. He sits at the front of church on a Sunday and does the actions to the songs enthusiastically.

What strikes me most about Myke is that he really loves those kids—he'd say that seeing them perform at our annual Christmas carol service, singing their little hearts out in nativity costumes, is one of the highlights of his year. In his own words: "Society might not value what I do, but God does, and that's all that matters".

I definitely want to be a little more like Myke.

It's not just the "church stuff" which is meaningful either. Everything—work, rest and play—is made meaningful when we do it for the glory of God.

Of course, it doesn't always feel like that. You may not always be able to see meaning as you cycle through the daily grind of eat, sleep, work, repeat. But that's OK. God sees, and God knows. And one day, once he's welcomed you home as his good and faithful servant, you'll be able to see how he wove each little and large investment of the gold he'd given you into his great plan—how he used what you did to build his eternity.

In a world in which everything else proves meaningless, that's meaning enough for me, for ever.

# 12. SELF-DOUBT

## WHAT IF I FAIL IN FRONT OF EVERYBODY?

"Know your limitations and be content with them. Too much ambition results in promotion to a job you can't do."

That's a quote from David Brent in *The Office*. But it could just as easily have come from the voice in my head (although the voice in my head isn't quite that witty).

I reckon—based on an unscientific survey of my friends and colleagues—that everyone hears a similar voice of self-doubt. Even the people who look the most confident do. For some of us the voice whispers; for others it shouts. For some it offers a daily running commentary; for others it offers occasional cutting critique.

But the voice is there, saying things like:

"You're going to fail in front of everyone."

"How on earth did you get this gig?"

"No one actually likes you. They're just hanging out with you because they feel sorry for you."

"Your family is going to be so disappointed."

"It will never happen, so don't bother trying."

"This is a bad idea and it's going to go horribly wrong."

As we start, I should lay my cards on the table and admit that I'm having doubts about writing this self-doubt chapter. (The irony is not lost on me.) In fact, I'm having doubts about this whole book. Right now in this moment, here are my three biggest fears, ranked from least to greatest:

1. No one will buy the book.

2. People will buy the book and read it and see all my inner thoughts.

3. People will buy the book and read it and see all my inner thoughts, and not like them.

As you can see, it's catch-22.

So what would you put in the gaps?

1.

2.

3.

Obviously, I don't know what it is that puts your voice of self-doubt into overdrive. It might be a job with targets you're sure you'll never meet or a manager you'll never satisfy. A girl or a guy you think you'll never be good enough for. A role at church that you know you're stuffing up, or that you're avoiding because you don't think you've got what it takes. Or just a vague but horrible sense, as you look at your day or at your future, that you're not cut out to handle it.

No one wants to live this way. We all know it's not the way to get stuff done in life. How do we conquer the voice of self-doubt in our heads?

## BEYOND THE TED TALKS

Maybe the solution is to watch more self-help TED talks on YouTube, or to share more inspirational quotes. We're told to believe in ourselves. We're told that we can do it, so don't be afraid. We're told to stop listening to the negative voices—to look in the mirror and tell ourselves that we're awesome.

But that doesn't work for long.

In fact, it *can't* work—because being told that you're awesome is part of the problem. You were raised in a culture that set the bar pretty high in terms of what you are expected to achieve in life. You're meant to be making a difference, feeling fulfilled, finding yourself, and being all that you can be. Plus, if you went to university or college, you've probably got huge debts to start repaying. It doesn't seem enough, like it did a generation or two ago, to work hard in a normal job in a small town, pay the bills, have a family, and serve your local church (and even those things may well seem out of your reach right now). Add to this the way that social media enables you to measure your achievements against other people's—and your inner feelings against other people's outer façades—and the voice of self-doubt just gets louder and louder.

Of course, this isn't just a quarter-life issue. So-called "Imposter Syndrome", where people feel like a fraud and fear being exposed, was first observed in the 1970s among high-powered company executives. But in our 20s and early 30s, there's still a lot of life ahead of us, and not much of a track record to look back on and feel confident about. We're still figuring out what we're good at, and still acquiring skills and knowledge and experience.

Which means that genuine humility is a good thing. Our generation (rightly or wrongly) has this reputation for wanting to bypass the hard work and get straight to the good stuff. It's right to humbly admit that we've got a lot to learn. But more often than not, the voice of self-doubt is driven by a fear of what other people think of us—we don't want to fail because we don't want to be seen to fail. This is the opposite of humility—it's an inverted sort of pride.

If the world's answer to our insecurity is "Look at yourself and tell yourself you're great", the Christian cliché answer tends to be "Look away from yourself and see that your God is great". I've never quite worked out how to actually do that, so I'm not going to tell you to do it. The truth is that you do need to look inward, but not at yourself. You need to look inward at the One who dwells in you.

## YOUNG GUY, BIG JOB

Paul wrote the letters of 1 and 2 Timothy to a young man with a big job. Timothy had been Paul's companion and assistant on several missionary journeys around the Mediterranean. But by AD 66, when Paul wrote 2 Timothy, Paul was in a prison cell in Rome, and Timothy was leading the church in Ephesus. It was a big task—Paul's first letter to him shows that Timothy needed to appoint elders, confront dangerous false teachers, order the church's worship, and work out a way to make sure the weakest sheep in the flock were cared for.

Reading between the lines, we can tell that Timothy feels woefully inadequate for the job. He's young, kind of sickly, and shy. As Paul starts his second letter to Timothy, he "recalls [his] tears" (2 Timothy 1 v 4)—the last time Paul saw his protégé, the poor guy was crying.

So if the circumstances in front of you feel so overwhelming that they sometimes push you to the point of tears, keep reading. In an era before self-help books, think of 2 Timothy as a self-help letter, but with a radically different focus than anything you'll find in a bookstore. In fact, this isn't self-help, but Spirit-help.

Paul starts by reminding Timothy that, however he feels, the Lord has been at work through the circumstances of his life to bring him "grace, mercy and peace" through faith in the gospel (1 v 2). And faith comes with a consequence. He's meant to use it:

> *For this reason I remind you to fan into flame the gift of*
> *God, which is in you through the laying on of my hands. For*
> *the Spirit God gave us does not make us timid, but gives us*
> *power, love and self-discipline. (v 6-7)*

Paul is probably talking about Timothy's special commissioning to be the minister of the church in Ephesus. While you and I don't have Timothy's specific spiritual gift, we do have the Spirit—and the Spirit gives a variety of spiritual gifts. No Christian is left off the gift-list (1 Corinthians 12). And actually, the greatest gift the Spirit gives is himself.

Don't miss this: if you have faith in Christ, then you have the Holy Spirit—one person of the triune God of the universe—living in you. In you! And it is relying on him that will help us fight self-doubt; or, as Paul calls it, "timidity".

Timidity says that we have nothing to contribute.

Timidity says that we'll never succeed.

Timidity says that we can't do it.

But the Spirit "gives us power, love and self-discipline" (2 Timothy 1 v 7).

Those are three words our culture wouldn't often put together, but Paul groups them for a very good reason. Power means that we can get hard things done; we can be courageous in the face of challenge and criticism. Love ensures that this never comes at the expense of others. Love doesn't trample over people to get to the top—love cares for other people more than it cares about gaining recognition. And self-discipline rules out a "can't do it, so I won't try" attitude. Self-discipline works hard and focuses. It guards us from hypocrisy, because we're fighting to be on the inside what we're seeking to change on the outside.

If you've got faith, you've got the Spirit of power, love and self-discipline. If you've got the Spirit, you've got something to contribute to your church, to your family, to your neighbours, to your workplace, and to the world. You might look at your own social skills or brain power or talents and feel woefully inadequate. But that's OK. It doesn't rely on you.

## TIME FOR THE NEWSPAPER TRICK

My parents have a real coal fireplace in their living room (like a woodburner, but vintage). There's an intense caveman rivalry within the family over who can lay and light The Best Fire. Chemical fire-lighting aids are a banned substance in this competition.

To be honest, my fire-lighting skills aren't up to much. Ten minutes after striking the first match, I'm usually left with a pile of smoking cardboard, slightly-blackened kindling, and still-cold coals. My 87-year-old grandad will look on from his armchair, shake his head, and declare that it's time to use The

Newspaper Trick. You take a few big pieces of newspaper and spread them across the top of the opening of the fireplace, leaving just a little gap at the bottom. This creates a vacuum effect, and a current of air whooshes up under the newspaper, so that the pile of smouldering cardboard and charred wood suddenly becomes a roaring fire.

This is something like what it means to "fan into flame the gift of God" (v 6). You may feel like a pathetic pile of smoking embers at the moment; but if the Spirit is in you, you are alight, however small that appears to your own eyes. Even the most faltering flame can become a roaring fire. But that does require some intentional flame-fanning—a Newspaper Trick—on our part. The Spirit has given you particular spiritual gifts. None of these gifts are worthless or random or useless, like a spiritual lucky-dip prize that gathers dust in a draw full of clutter. Each gift has been lovingly given especially to you, so that you can use it "for the common good" of those around you (1 Corinthians 12 v 7).

So time for some self-reflection. Let's start with the negative—the whole area of fear.

In what ways are you being timid?

What is it that you're secretly too scared to take on?

Where do you let fear hold you back?

One rule I've tried to live by for the last decade is that I will never not do something because I'm afraid. Fear of other people is not a good motive for anything. A social situation that makes me nervous; a project at work that I'm scared of; a job at church that makes me hesitant—if I clock that the reason I'm about to say no is only fear, I'm going to say yes. Perhaps it's a good rule for you to take on for yourself.

Next, think about those three qualities of the Spirit—power, love and self-discipline.

What would they look like in this situation that makes you feel fearful?

Where do you need the Spirit's power?

Where do you need the Spirit's love?

Where do you need the Spirit's self-discipline?

Don't just note where you need it—ask for it. If there's a spiritual equivalent to The Newspaper Trick, it's a prayerful attitude of striving to "keep in step with the Spirit" (Galatians 5 v 25); of asking him every day to set the pace and direction of our day, and following where he leads.

Now, reflect on how you're gifted.

What are you good at?

In what areas has God particularly gifted you?

Your self-doubt might be blinding you to it—but it's probably obvious to the people who know you well. So ask them, and let them encourage you. And then, when you have an idea of what those gifts are, work out how you can start fanning them. But I'll give you a clue to start you off—most of the time, we grow in our gifts by using our gifts.

The aim is self-awareness, not self-doubt. There's a difference. Self-doubt says, "I'm bad at this, I'll always be bad at this, and I'm afraid because I know that sooner or later everyone else is going to think I'm bad at this." This attitude is not helpful. Self-awareness says, "I think I'm spiritually gifted in this area, and even though it terrifies me, I'm going to start stepping out in the Spirit's power, and see what God may do in me and through me. I won't be perfect, but I'm ready to learn. And if it doesn't work out, that's OK, because I wasn't finding my value in being great at this anyway."

This attitude is life-changing. When we speak fearful self-criticism to ourselves, we pour cold water all over the embers of God's gift to us. But when we speak prayerfully to our Father, acknowledging our weakness and asking for his Spirit to work in us, the fire burns stronger. Self-doubt causes us to settle, but self-awareness moves us to grow—to keep fanning those flames.

So whatever your gifts and whatever your fears—it's time for The Newspaper Trick.

## BE MORE DRAGON

OK, we're ready to start fanning. But what exactly does the Spirit make us powerful to do? Is it true what they told us at school, that "you can do anything if you believe"—as long as the thing we're believing in is the Spirit?

Paul explains what the Spirit's power is for in 2 Timothy 1 v 14:

> Guard the good deposit that was entrusted to you—guard it with the help of the Holy Spirit who lives in us.

The image is a bit like a dragon's hoard of treasure in a cave (for the purposes of this analogy, the dragon's a goodie). Raiders keep trying to break in and steal what they can—seeking to chip away at the stash gem by gem or goblet by goblet. Some of those raiders come with all guns blazing. Others sneak in under a disguise.

But standing in the cave to protect the treasure is... you. And you're not a weed with a sword that's so heavy you can barely lift it. You've got "the help of the Holy Spirit who lives in [you]" (v 14).

And that makes you a dragon.

Not only that, but the Spirit is working in you to make you *more* dragon—sharpening your teeth, toughening up your scales, fine-tuning your instincts.

The "good deposit" is the good news—the gospel. And you've got it. So be on your guard. Don't let other people distract you from following Jesus and serving his people. Keep growing in holiness, because that's what God has called you to (v 9). Be a "herald" who declares the good news to others (v 11). Learn to screen out the raiders who try to undermine what God has said ("Surely God means..." "I like to think that..." "How can it be wrong if...?"). Take seriously your responsibility to yourself and to your friends at church to keep them on the straight and narrow. Go to every Bible study seeking to speak truth. Gently challenge flawed thinking about the world and the word. Learn the art of asking the kind of questions that get an honest answer. You can do all of these things because you "have the help of the Holy Spirit who lives in [you]". Be more dragon.

Remember, too, what you're guarding: the gospel. I'm not sure we're very good at grasping just how good the good news is. Paul reminds us:

> *He has saved us and called us to a holy life—not because of anything we have done but because of his own purpose and grace. This grace was given us in Christ Jesus before the beginning of time, but it has now been revealed through the appearing of our Saviour, Christ Jesus, who has destroyed death and has brought life and immortality to light through the gospel. (v 9-10)*

The treasure you're guarding is the very thing which addresses your self-doubt.

The voice of self-doubt says, *You'll never amount to anything much*. The gospel says, *You don't need to. Christ has done everything.* We didn't get the job of "Christian" because we presented him with our résumés, talked up our experience in an interview and blagged ourselves a spot on his team—and so we now need to prove that we can do it.

No, Christ knew exactly who we were when he took us on—with all our weaknesses and sin and mess. He chose to love us "not because of anything we have done"—he loved us "before the beginning of time", so it can't possibly be because of who we are. It's because of who he is: unrelentingly gracious, and determined to prove it to people like us. And however we may stuff up in the future, this grace isn't something which can be taken away, because Christ has already done in the past all that needed to be done. He "destroyed death" through his own death and resurrection, and has given us "life" now and "immortality" later. We're not on probation. So loosen the internal knots and enjoy being on the team. There's nothing to prove, nothing to earn. We've already been given the grace that matters. And when we grasp the truth that God accepts us and loves us and is rooting for us in Christ, then the opinion of others—and even our opinion of ourselves—will matter far, far less.

So much of our self-doubt is about a fear of failure. Deep down, we're desperate to succeed. Self-doubt tells us we never will (or at least that we likely won't), and that's what makes it so crushing. And the voice of self-doubt will continue to crush us if we're ultimately looking for a different kind of "success" than the simple aim of guarding this treasure. The Christian life doesn't usually look like having the rest of the world think you've made it. Self-doubt will crush us if we load the weight of the world's pressure—to perform well, to please others, to be winning at life—onto our own shoulders.

What frees us from that burden is saying, "I'm not powerful, but the Spirit is. I can't do it, but the Spirit can through me. I will stumble and fail, but that's OK because my approval and worth and purpose were never up to me to create or earn or maintain; Christ has loved me from the beginning of time, and has brought me light and life in the gospel."

It's time for you and me to step out in faith—to live as though the Spirit is stronger than our self-doubts. And see what happens. Tim Chester puts it like this in his book *Enjoying God*:

> "If you want to see the Spirit at work in your life, then attempt things that you feel you can't do without his help. Everything we do for God is done with the Spirit's help, whether we feel it or not. But if you want to feel the Spirit's help, then attempt things that feel beyond you. Do not complain that God never does anything dramatic in your life if you never attempt anything outside your comfort zone."
>
> *(page 119)*

You're not a no-hoper. You're not doomed to fail. You've got the Spirit and that means you're a dragon.

## WHEN I AM WEAK...

One of the advantages of working for a Christian company is that, on the whole, your boss is pretty nice and sometimes gives you good advice.

I started off working for The Good Book Company (a Christian publisher) as an intern, first for six months, and then for another six. When they offered to keep me on permanently, I was euphoric. A real job with a real salary. Less tea-making and more responsibility. I felt like I had made it.

The feeling didn't last long. I can remember a meeting I had with my new boss where he outlined exactly what the role was going to look like, and we set some goals for me for the year ahead.

"I'm so excited," he declared. I wasn't.

"I can't wait to see where you take this role," he enthused. I could.

"You're going to be great," he exclaimed. "I have every confidence in you." I didn't.

I was terrified.

He could tell.

"Are you alright?" he asked. "You seem a bit..."

"I just..." I stammered. "It's just whenever I'm told to do something, my first thought is always, 'I can't do it'."

"Listen," he said, "sometimes I wish I was a can't-do person. I go into things thinking I can do everything, and then find I can't. But when you think you can't do things, that's good, if you let it drive you to being more prayerfully dependent on God. When you feel overwhelmed, let that cause you to pray about it."

The irony is that we had almost exactly the same conversation again in another situation two years later—I don't think he'd remembered the first one, but I had. I knew it; I was just struggling to live it.

And I still struggle. I still waver between proud, prayerless self-confidence and paralysing, prayerless self-doubt. You can tell my problem, and my solution: I don't pray, and I need to pray.

Self-doubt is helpful *when we know what to do with it*. Weakness leads to strength, and fear turns to confidence, if we rely on Christ's power. Before he could write that letter to Timothy, that's what Paul had to learn for himself:

> [The Lord] said to me, "My grace is sufficient for you, for my power is made perfect in weakness." Therefore I will boast all the more gladly about my weaknesses, so that Christ's power may rest on me. That is why, for Christ's sake, I delight in weaknesses, in insults, in hardships, in persecutions, in difficulties. For when I am weak, then I am strong.
> (2 Corinthians 12 v 9-10)

When self-doubt strikes, you can agree with the voice in your head that tells you you're not able. And then you can look to the Spirit and ask him to go to work. And then you can go to work. For when you are weak, and dependent, and prayerful, then you are strong.

# OUTRO

## THIS JUST ISN'T HOW I IMAGINED LIFE WOULD GO

If you could give your former self a tour of your life now, what would they make of it?

I reckon 16-year-old me would be pleasantly surprised at how some things have panned out. She'd be intrigued by the new cast of faces around me. She'd be relieved that nothing's gone majorly wrong. She'd be astonished to have written an actual, real, proper book—especially one that someone kept reading all the way to page 199 (high five to us both!).

But I suspect that my teenage self would be quietly disappointed that, overall, adult life feels very ordinary. 26 and single in suburbia—I don't know quite what teenage me was expecting as she stood ready to launch into adulthood, but it wasn't this. Is this it? It just isn't how I imagined life would go.

And that, so often, is the problem. The Quarter-Life Crisis is triggered when the gap between what we imagined and what we have grows so wide that we find ourselves free-falling down it.

But there's hope at the bottom of the chasm, because ready to catch us is a God with a bigger imagination than ours. Even if

"GOD'S SCRIPT FOR OUR LIVES
IS NEVER LESS THAN WHAT WE
IMAGINED – IT IS ALWAYS
IMMEASURABLY MORE."

#ISTHISIT

adult life isn't going how you imagined, God has promised to do more than you imagined with it:

> *Now to him who is able to do immeasurably more than*
> *all we ask or imagine, according to his power that is at*
> *work within us, to him be glory in the church and in Christ*
> *Jesus throughout all generations, for ever and ever! Amen.*
> (*Ephesians 3 v 20-21*)

## MY LIFE, THE SITCOM

I have a friend who likes to think of his life in terms of "narrative arcs". It works like this: imagine your life is a long-running sitcom. Plots and subplots weave together—they come to the fore or fade to the background; some get nicely resolved while others reach a dead end. Characters come and go for seasons at a time. There are plot twists, dramatic climaxes, agonising choices, and satisfying all's-well-that-ends-well moments. There are funny and ridiculous clips that you want to re-watch again and again—and there are sad ones that make you cry every time. There are different scenes and episodes and seasons. ("Today has the feeling of a season finale to it," my friend once declared on our way to a wedding—and, to be fair to him, it was.)

Seeing the bigger story helps him make sense of the ordinariness of his day-to-day existence. It's a way of seeing the direction of travel, if only, sometimes, in hindsight. It reminds him that however much he doesn't like his current situation, "for now" is not for ever; it's only ever for now. Ultimately, it's a way of stepping back to enjoy the details of God's providence—to rejoice in knowing the script is being written by somebody else.

I'll bet your "narrative arc" hasn't gone the way your 16-year-old self would have written it. But God's script for our lives is never less than what we imagined—it is always immeasurably more.

Your life is not a second-rate sitcom with you as the title character, that runs its course and then gets cut. If you have eyes to see it, your life is immeasurably better than that.

The *purpose* is immeasurably grander. Your existence is not at all meaningless. It's not a search for happiness or satisfaction that will end in disappointment. Your life's purpose is this: "To [God] be glory" (v 21). God has written a script that reveals his glory—that shows the weighty, awesome essence of who he is: a God of justice, grace, compassion, commitment and complete integrity. And God doesn't just show us how wonderful he is, like we're audience members watching a performance. Instead, he invites us onto the stage to live lives that marvel at and enjoy how wonderful he is—to give him glory. It's being part of this performance that will make our hearts beat. And at the end of time, we'll trace the storyline and stand in awe of God's creativity and grace.

The *means* are immeasurably bigger. God shows his glory, so that he can be enjoyed and praised "in the church and in Christ Jesus". The way that God is putting his power and goodness on display is by saving people—lots of people—through the death and resurrection of Christ Jesus. It's about more and more people experiencing "the boundless riches of Christ" so that "now, *through the church*, the manifold wisdom of God should be made known" (v 10, my italics). Your life isn't about what you can achieve or acquire—it's about playing your small part in this bigger story to display and enjoy God's glory. You and I are just two saved souls among many—but it is the fact that there are *so* many that is so exciting.

And the *timeline* is immeasurably longer. Your story won't end in 50 or 60 years (or less), because you're part of a plot that started before you were born and that will go on for much longer. It's a story that's not just for millennials or Generation Z—God will be glorified "throughout all generations, for ever and ever".

Which means that today, the *power at work in you* is immeasurably stronger than your own. You might feel a little bit weak and lost and lonely. You might be frustrated or sad that you can't make your life go in the direction you want. But God is the one "who is able to do immeasurably more than all we ask or imagine, according to his power that is at work within us". He's working all the circumstances of your life to bring him glory in ways that you could never dream up and may not even be able to see. He's answering your prayers in ways that go above and beyond what you expect.

Sure, your part in the grand story of the universe is pretty small. But don't complain about the part you've been given. Marvel that you've been given a part at all. God doesn't need you to bring him glory—he lets you bring him glory. Don't miss how incredibly personal this is either. We're talking about a big God with a big plan—but he's a big God who is at work within *you*.

When *this* is the story we're excited about, it closes the gap between what we imagine and what we have. With this perspective, we won't be in free-fall for long—because it's in this big story that we find the joy, meaning and purpose that we crave.

So for the rest of our 20s and our 30s and the decades beyond, let this be our anthem:

> *Now to him who is able to do immeasurably more than all*
> *we ask or imagine, according to his power that is at work*
> *within us, to him be glory in the church and in Christ Jesus*
> *throughout all generations, for ever and ever! Amen.*

# EXTRA RESOURCES

This book scratches the surface on a whole range of topics. To dig a little deeper or get more help, here are some good places to start. (I make no apology that the majority of them come from The Good Book Company!)

## DISSATISFACTION
*Dealing with Disappointment* by John Hindley (TGBC, 2017)
*Chasing Contentment* by Erik Raymond (Crossway, 2017)

## DECISION PARALYSIS
*Just Do Something* by Kevin DeYoung (Moody, 2009)
*The Defining Decade* by Meg Jay (Canongate, 2016)—a secular book, but definitely stimulating

## ROOTLESSNESS
*Keeping Place* by Jen Pollock Michel (IVP, 2017)
*Why Bother with Church?* by Sam Allberry (TGBC, 2016)

## NOSTALGIA AND REGRET
For nostalgia, just steer clear of Buzzfeed and you'll be OK.

## I HATE MY JOB
*Every Good Endeavour* by Tim Keller (Viking/Hodder Faith, 2012)
On slavery in the Bible, "Why it's wrong to say the Bible is pro-slavery" by Gavin Ortlund (www.thegospelcoalition.org/article/why-wrong-say-bible-pro-slavery, accessed 13/09/18) or *Is God a Moral Monster?* by Paul Copan (Baker, 2011)

## DOUBT
*The Reason for God* by Tim Keller (Penguin Books, 2009)
*How Can I Be Sure?* by John Stevens (TGBC, 2014)
On the Bible, *Can I Really Trust the Bible?* by Barry Cooper (TGBC, 2014) or *Why Trust the Bible?* by Amy Orr-Ewing (IVP, 2005)

On the problem of suffering, *If I were God, I'd End All the Pain* by John Dickson (Matthias Media, 2001) or *Where Was God When That Happened?* by Christopher Ash (TGBC, 2017)

On science, *Can Science Explain Everything?* by John Lennox (TGBC, 2019) or *Unnatural Enemies* by Kirsten Birkett (Matthias Media, 1997)

On "hard teaching" about sexuality and gender, *Is God Anti-Gay?* by Sam Allberry (TGBC, 2013), or *God and the Transgender Debate* by Andrew Walker (TGBC, 2017)

## LONELINESS
*True Friendship* by Vaughan Roberts (10ofthose, 2013)
*Real* by Catherine Parks (TGBC, 2018)
*You Can Really Grow* by John Hindley (TGBC, 2015—some great stuff on reading the Bible)

## SINGLENESS
*7 Myths about Singleness* by Sam Allberry (Crossway, 2019)

## DATING AND MARRIAGE
*Not Yet Married* by Marshall Segal (Crossway, 2017)
*The Meaning of Marriage* by Tim and Kathy Keller (Dutton, 2011)
*Gospel Centred Marriage* by Tim Chester (TGBC, 2011)
*James For You* by Sam Allberry (TGBC, 2015)

## GETTING OLD
Those suffering physically might appreciate *Hope When It Hurts* by Kristen Wetherell and Sarah Walton (TGBC, 2016)

## MEANINGLESSNESS
*Serving without Sinking* by John Hindley (TGBC, 2013)—a really great book for those who feel stuck in the weekly grind of church life

## SELF-DOUBT
*Enjoying God* by Tim Chester (TGBC, 2018)
*The Freedom of Self-Forgetfulness* by Tim Keller (10ofthose, 2012)
*Unstuck* by Tim Lane (TGBC, 2019)

# THANK YOU TO...

... the many friends (and some near strangers) who gave me a slice of their thoughts in aid of this book, and who appear in it under a range of pseudonyms. Special thanks to Michael, who's given more slices than most over the years; and to the Platt girls, whose honesty got this book started, and finished.

... those who gave feedback on parts of the manuscript: Nathan, Sam, Ruth, Emma, Liz, Catherine and "Captain Feedback" Dan. Thank you too to the excellent Linda Allcock and her team of reviewers from The Globe Church, London: Alice, Sarah, Wing, Tara and Ryan.

... The Good Book Company. I guess I have a better idea than most authors quite how many people it takes to get these words from my screen, onto paper, and into your hands— thank you, all. Special thanks to André Parker for his game-changing avocado cover design; and to Carl Laferton, who believed in this book (and its author) even when I didn't, and made it so much better with his comments and edits.

... the whole Chessington Evangelical Church family, for teaching me and looking after me in so many ways. So many of you have shown interest in the progress of this project (and patience at my endless refrain of, "Well, as I say in my book..."). Shout out to my Hub group and the Fusion team who endure me week by week and make serving so much fun.

... the Jones family, for all your love and encouragement. Big love to my siblings Matt, Martha and Tim, and the outlaws, Bel and Dan. And I owe the greatest debt of gratitude to my parents, Mark and Isabel—thank you for shaping me into the adult I am through two decades of faithful, godly parenting (and for helping me survive as an adult through phone support on everything from life decisions to bike maintenance).

# thegoodbook
## COMPANY

**BIBLICAL | RELEVANT | ACCESSIBLE**

At The Good Book Company, we are dedicated to helping Christians and local churches grow. We believe that God's growth process always starts with hearing clearly what he has said to us through his timeless word—the Bible.

Ever since we opened our doors in 1991, we have been striving to produce Bible-based resources that bring glory to God. We have grown to become an international provider of user-friendly resources to the Christian community, with believers of all backgrounds and denominations using our books, Bible studies, devotionals, evangelistic resources, and DVD-based courses.

We want to equip ordinary Christians to live for Christ day by day, and churches to grow in their knowledge of God, their love for one another, and the effectiveness of their outreach.

Call us for a discussion of your needs or visit one of our local websites for more information on the resources and services we provide.

Your friends at The Good Book Company

thegoodbook.com | thegoodbook.co.uk
thegoodbook.com.au | thegoodbook.co.nz
thegoodbook.co.in